Elementary Data Analysis Using Microsoft Excel

Anita M. Meehan, Ph. D.

Kutztown University

C. Bruce Warner, Ph. D.

Kutztown University

Mc Graw Hill

Boston   Burr Ridge, IL   Dubuque, IA   Madison, WI   New York   San Francisco   St. Louis
Bangkok   Bogotá   Caracas   Lisbon   London   Madrid
Mexico City   Milan   New Delhi   Seoul   Singapore   Sydney   Taipei   Toronto

McGraw-Hill Higher Education

A Division of The McGraw·Hill Companies

ELEMENTARY DATA ANALYSIS USING MICROSOFT EXCEL

 This book is printed on recycled, acid-free paper containing 10% postconsumer waste.

5 6 7 8 9 QPD 04 03 02

ISBN 0–07–236051–8

Editorial director: *Jane E. Vaicunas*
Executive editor: *Joseph Terry*
Editorial assistant: *Barbara Santoro*
Senior marketing manager: *James Rozsa*
Project manager: *Sheila M. Frank*
Production supervisor: *Enboge Chong*
Designer: *Rick Noel*
Typeface: *11/13 Times Roman*
Printer: *Quebecor Printing Book Group/Dubuque, IA*

www.mhhe.com

Table of Contents

Preface

Why Excel?

Who among us hasn't heard students lament: "It's bad enough we have to take statistics. Why do we have to learn this software, too?" Like many other instructors in the social and behavioral sciences, for years we relied primarily on specialized statistical software like SPSS (Statistical Package for the Social Sciences) in our statistics and research methods courses. As computer technology has become ubiquitous and spreadsheet programs more and more popular, we wondered if there weren't a better way. This led us to use—with pleasing results—Microsoft Excel, a popular spreadsheet software package, in our introductory statistics course.

Why use a spreadsheet application like Microsoft Excel? There are two main reasons we embraced the use of spreadsheets over specialized packages such as SPSS.

Simpler data manipulation. With a spreadsheet application like Excel, students can concentrate more on statistical concepts and outcomes and less on the mechanics of the software. Data entry is generally recognized as easier than in specialized statistical software. One reason for this is that many students today are already familiar with spreadsheets; if they are not versed in Excel, they understand basic spreadsheet functions. Even for students who have no previous experience, spreadsheets are generally easier to learn than specialized software. This, in turn, reduces the time and energy that instructors spend on training both inside and outside the classroom. Using a well-known application rather than specialized software also means that students have multiple sources of technical support if they encounter difficulty completing an assignment.

Generalized skills. Using spreadsheet software better achieves our educational mission of providing students with skills that are generalizable, transferable, and marketable after the statistics course is long over. Perhaps because of this, we have noticed that students have a more positive attitude about working with Excel than with SPSS. They readily see its real-world applicability, are aware that it is a computer skill valued by employers, and are more willing to tolerate some of the frustrations they encounter.

There are several other benefits that we have found to using Excel over SPSS:

- **Output format.** Commonly used specialized statistical programs generate detailed output that is meant for advanced users, not beginners. Our experience has been that such sophisticated output causes added confusion and headaches for students and instructors. In contrast, the output generated by Excel is more basic; its content is similar to problem solutions shown in introductory statistics textbook exercises or during classroom instruction.
- **Economic benefits.** Most students and universities already own or have access to computers with spreadsheet software, whereas specialized statistical programs are an added expense. Microsoft Excel is a natural choice for a statistics course, as it performs most basic analyses, creates easily customizable graphs of professional quality, and is a market leader in its product category.
- **Industry support.** A number of individuals have written statistical add-ins and simulations that enhance Excel's capabilities. Some of these are free to download via the Internet. Good starting points for Excel resources can be found at the Web site of the Association of Statistics Specialists Using Microsoft Excel (http://www.mailbase.ac.uk/lists/assume/) and at Spreadsheets in Education (http://sunsite.univie.ac.at/Spreadsite/).

Why This Book?

Teaching with Excel was an improvement on teaching with SPSS, but we still felt that our students needed a reference guide to help them. Numerous Excel manuals are available to help learn the spreadsheet program, but none are geared to teaching statistics and research methods. So, like many instructors, we prepared our own course handouts. Since then, when we have come across the few books written for teaching statistics with Excel, they are primarily oriented toward schools of business, which have a long history of using spreadsheets.

If the business school can do it, why not the social sciences? We made the decision to publish our handouts in the form of this book—it's unique in that it was written to include procedures and examples relevant to data analysis in the social and behavioral sciences. We included what we think are typical topics covered in an introductory statistics course, which brings us to another important point: This book is most useful as a *supplement* to textbooks in introductory statistics or research methods because our goal is to show students how to carry out data analysis in Excel *without* inundating them with statistical formulas and theory.

Because Excel's built-in data analysis tools are limited, advanced courses in statistics and more involved statistical procedures will require specialized software. We prefer to use SPSS for Windows in such cases. Fortunately, data files can be exchanged easily between Excel and other applications. In *Appendix A,* we specifically describe how to exchange files between Excel and SPSS, and we provide insights into how Excel files could be imported into other applications.

What Have We Included?

The handouts that this book is based on have been student-tested on several classes, and we wrote them assuming no prior knowledge of Excel. Except for the first two chapters explaining how to install the Analysis ToolPak and perform basic functions in Excel, each chapter is intended to stand more or less alone. This way, instructors can tailor the book to their specific courses. At the end of each chapter, we include exercises that provide students with practice in both statistics and Excel.

The chapters focusing on specific statistical procedures include an overview of when and why each procedure would be performed, plus research examples, steps for the procedure, and interpretation of the output. Copious screen shots (these show exactly what you will see on your computer's monitor at various steps in the sequence) are used for clarity and for navigational purposes. We don't want anyone to get lost—conceptually or sequentially—while performing a procedure or interpreting its output.

Several chapters are devoted to the visual display of data using bar charts, histograms, scatterplots, and line charts. Our intent with these chapters is to help students learn how graphs can improve the understanding of data, as well as teach them to produce their own presentation-quality figures for oral and written reports. Instructors who are interested in having students generate graphs and figures that conform to the publication style of the American Psychological Association will need to make some modifications to our instructions.

Readers need to note that this guide was prepared using Microsoft Excel 97 operating under Windows 95. For those using another version of Excel for Windows or for the MacIntosh, the screen images and menus will look slightly different, but the basic spreadsheet functionality will be the same.

Acknowledgments

Though computer technology has its frustrating moments, our students have responded favorably to using Excel for their assignments, and they see its benefits. Their feedback has been invaluable in helping us to improve this guide. In particular, we wish to thank our undergraduate statistics and Excel tutor, Megan Mumma, for her assistance. Our colleague, John Vafeas, tested the first draft with his classes and offered helpful advice.

The support of our editors at McGraw-Hill was instrumental in helping this book come to fruition, so we would like to thank Joseph Terry, Executive Editor, Fred Speers, Editorial Assistant, and Sarah Dunn, Freelance Editor. We are also grateful to the reviewers for their suggestions and input: **Philip Tolin**, Central Washington University; **Kerri Pickel**, Ball State University; **Dan Moriarty**, University of San Diego; **Richard Wielkiewicz**, College of St. Benedict; and **David Pittenger**, Marietta College. We also wish to acknowledge that initial work on this project was supported by funding we received from Kutztown University.

Anita M. Meehan
C. Bruce Warner

Installing Excel's Data Analysis ToolPak

In addition to using spreadsheet formulas for calculations, Excel comes with a basic set of built-in mathematical and statistical functions. Excel also contains an add-in for expanded statistical capabilities called the **Analysis ToolPak**. These data analysis tools are not part of the typical installation of Excel, so you may need to install them on your computer. Most users will need to perform only Steps 1 and 2 to accomplish this task.

Installation Steps

Step 1: Check for Prior Analysis ToolPak Installation

- Start Excel.
- Click on the **Tools** menu.
- See if there is a choice called **Data Analysis** listed near the bottom of the **Tools** menu. If so, the **Analysis ToolPak** is already installed on your computer. There is no need to move on to Step 2.

Step 2: Install the Analysis ToolPak

- Highlight and click on **Add-ins**, as shown in Figure 1.1.
- Check the box next to the phrase **Analysis ToolPak** when the **Add-ins** dialog box appears (see Figure 1.2). If you do not see **Analysis ToolPak** listed as an add-in option, go to Step 3 now.
- Click on the **OK** button.
- Wait for the data analysis tools to install.
- Click on the **Tools** menu and verify that the installation was completed successfully. A choice called **Data Analysis** should appear near the bottom of the **Tools** menu. If so, you are finished and there is no need to move on to Step 3. If not, repeat Step 2; something probably went wrong during the installation process.

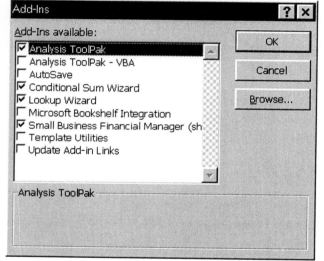

Figure 1.1
Selecting Add-Ins
on the Tools
menu.

Figure 1.2
Check the
Analysis ToolPak
box in the Add-Ins
dialog box.

Step 3: Install the Analysis ToolPak to the Add-ins List

During Step 2, if you did not see **Analysis ToolPak** listed as an option, it means this add-in does not reside on your computer. You need to run Microsoft Excel's **Setup** program, which enables you to install additional components.

- Insert your Excel CD-ROM or floppy disk. If you have your CD-ROM's auto-play feature turned on, Microsoft's **Setup** program should automatically activate when the CD-ROM is inserted so you can skip to the last bulleted item in Step 3. Otherwise, you need to:
- Go to the Windows 95 **Start** menu.
- Choose **Run.**
- Type the drive letter of your Excel CD-ROM or disk location followed by the word **setup** (For example: **d:setup** or **a:setup**).
- Choose to install Microsoft Excel when the first **Setup** screen appears.

- Choose **Add/Remove** components when a screen similar to that shown in Figure 1.3 appears.
- Continue to follow the **Setup** procedure's screen choices to select the Excel component to install, which is the **Analysis Toolpak Add-in**. Refer to an Excel manual or Excel's **Help Menu** (look under **add-ins**) if you need assistance in running the **Setup** program and installing the component.

Figure 1.3
Microsoft Excel
97 Setup dialog
box.

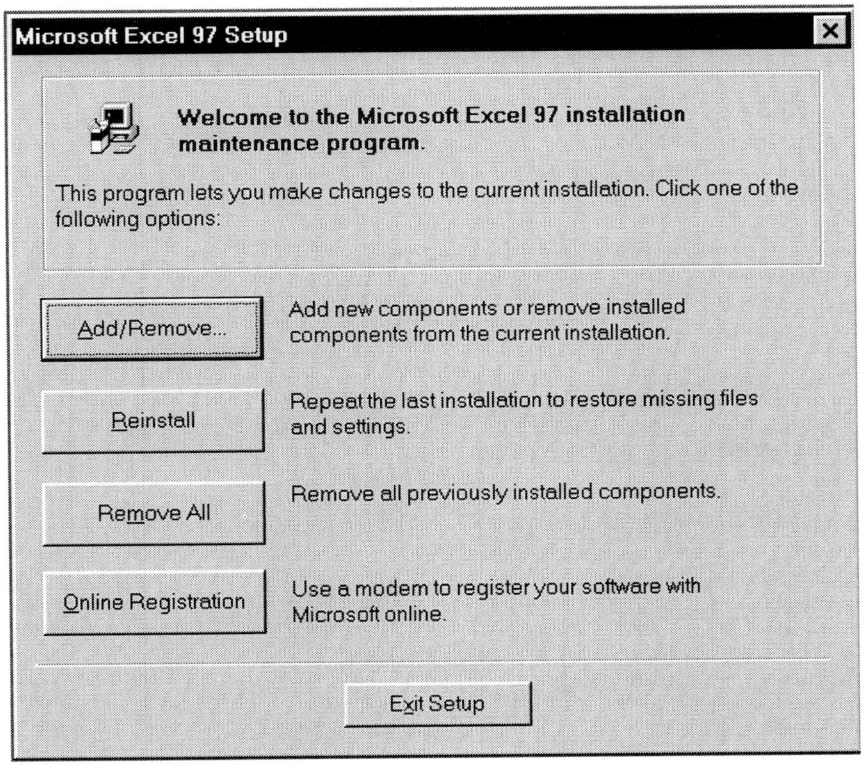

Step 4: Install the Analysis ToolPak to the Tools Menu

The **Analysis ToolPak Add-In** resides on your computer after successfully running **Setup**, but the tools are not yet available as a menu item in Excel.
- Start Excel.
- Perform Step 2 to finish the installation of the **Analysis ToolPak**.

Spreadsheet Basics

When you start Excel, the first thing you see is a window containing a blank workbook. The appearance of Excel and the workbook window may vary from start-up to start-up, depending upon the states they were in when the program was last used. Nevertheless, the screen image should resemble the one in Figure 2.1. We will refer to the features labeled in Figure 2.1 at various points in this chapter.

Figure 2.1
Basic
components of
Excel.

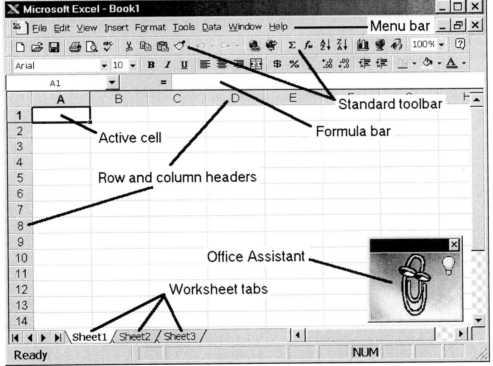

In this introduction, we make a few basic assumptions:
- You already know how to use basic Windows controls (scroll bars; the minimize, maximize, restore, and close buttons).
- You know how to resize windows.
- You understand mouse button usage.

> **Note:** Throughout this book, we use the term *primary* mouse button instead of *left* mouse button, and the term *secondary* mouse button instead of *right* mouse button. (This is because left-handed users often reverse the functions of the left and right keys of the mouse.) The primary mouse button is used for selection, and the secondary mouse button is used for bringing up context menus.

As we proceed through this introduction and this manual, remember that multiple ways exist to perform almost every task. For experienced users, this flexibility is a definite bonus. Unfortunately, for novice users, having multiple ways of doing everything can be frustrating. We sympathize, and we have tried to provide the one best, most efficient way to perform a task whenever possible.

What Is a Spreadsheet?

At its simplest, a spreadsheet is the software equivalent of a paper spreadsheet or ledger originally used for accounting. Essentially a spreadsheet consists of a matrix of cells with row and column headers. Columns are labeled with letters, and rows are labeled with numbers. Individual cells are identified by their column and row headings. For example, the upper left cell is A1, the one immediately to the right is B1, and so on.

Like their paper counterparts, the cells of software spreadsheets can hold numbers or labels. Unlike their paper counterparts, the cells of software spreadsheets can also hold formulas, which begin with an equal sign. A simple example is:

=A1+B1

Entering this formula into a cell results in the cell always displaying the sum of cells A1 and B1; if the value in either A1 or B1 should change, this cell's value will also change.

As we will discover, Excel can do much more than simple arithmetic. This book will teach you how to use formulas, produce charts, and perform statistical analyses with the **Analysis ToolPak**, which is Excel's standard statistical add-in.

Methods for Performing Statistical Analyses in Excel

Excel provides us with three tools for performing statistical analyses: (1) formulas and functions, (2) the **Analysis ToolPak**, and (3) **Chart Wizard**. Each has its advantages and uses, and we will show you how and when to use each appropriately.

Formulas and functions. Excel has the capability to solve both simple and complex equations. **Paste Function** f_* simplifies the use of functions by taking you through the steps necessary to paste statistical calculations into your spreadsheet. We will show you how to use **Paste Function** to find statistics such as mean, median, mode, standard deviation, variance, and correlation.

Analysis ToolPak. Once you have performed the simple steps that install this add-in feature as a working part of your Excel spreadsheet, you will have an array of tools for performing descriptive statistics, *t*-tests, analysis of variance, correlation, and regression at your fingertips. It also adds statistical and graphing capabilities that are unavailable in the basic Excel application. (See *Chapter 1* for instructions on installing this feature).

Chart Wizard. Excel is also an excellent application for graphing data. We will describe how to create bar charts, histograms, line charts, and scatterplots using Excel's **Chart Wizard** 📊, along with the **Analysis ToolPak**.

> **A note on versions of Excel: Paste Function** and **Analysis ToolPak** operate similarly across different versions of Excel. However, readers who are using earlier software versions should be aware that Microsoft made numerous improvements to the charting package for Excel 97. Most charting features available in Excel 97 are available in earlier editions of Excel, but others, such as variable-size plotting symbols, are unavailable. The sequence of **Chart Wizard** steps may vary. Also, be aware that **Paste Function** was known as **Function Wizard** in previous versions of Excel.

Getting Help

Help is always nearby if you know where to look. The four primary means of getting help are:

1. Clicking on the **Help** entry on the **Menu Bar** at the top of the Excel application (Figure 2.1).
2. Clicking on the Office Assistant (Figures 2.1 and 2.2).
3. Clicking on the Office Assistant icon ❓ on the **Standard Toolbar** (Figure 2.1).
4. Pressing **F1** on the keyboard.

Sometimes the **Office Assistant** will spontaneously ask if you need help with a particular feature, as shown in Figure 2.2. Respond by clicking on one of the alternatives provided. If you desire more help, the **Office Assistant** will respond by offering a menu of choices. (You can also ignore **Office Assistant** if you require no help).

Figure 2.2
Office Assistant
offering help.

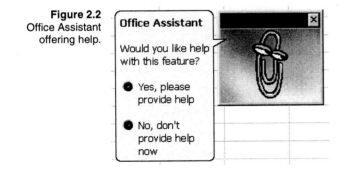

Working with Spreadsheets

Selecting Spreadsheets

Excel organizes spreadsheets into workbooks. Each workbook occupies a separate window in the application and saves to a separate file on disk. By default, Excel will start with one fresh workbook that contains three blank spreadsheet pages. The pages are named *Sheet 1, Sheet 2,* and *Sheet 3*.

> **Tips:**
> - To open a new workbook, choose **New** from the **File** menu, or click the ☐ icon on the **Standard Toolbar**.
> - Choose **Arrange** from the **Window** menu to arrange multiple workbooks visually on screen. (**Tiled** in the **Arrange Windows** dialog box is a good choice if you wish to lay out two or more open workbooks side-by-side).

You can select a spreadsheet by clicking its tab at the bottom of the page. To become familiar with moving from sheet to sheet, position your mouse pointer on one of the tabs and click; try it on each of the tabs.

Go back to the first sheet (*Sheet 1*). Click the secondary mouse button while holding the pointer over the *Sheet 1* tab. A context menu will appear, as shown in Figure 2.3. This menu gives you several options:

- **Insert** allows you to add worksheets to your file.
- **Delete** will eliminate the current worksheet (the one whose tab is highlighted).
- **Rename** allows you to name the current worksheet something more meaningful than just a number.
- **Move or Copy** allows you to move or copy worksheets to other workbooks, or create copies within the current workbook.
- **Select All Sheets** allows you to select all of the sheets in the current workbook, so that you may manipulate them all simultaneously.

Press the **Esc** key on the keyboard to close the context menu.

Figure 2.3
The context menu of the worksheet tab.

Insert...
Delete
Rename
Move or Copy...
Select All Sheets
View Code

Tip: Keep in mind that context menus are available throughout Excel. When you want to alter or customize any feature, click the secondary mouse button and check out your available options on the context menu that appears.

Selecting Cells and Moving Around Within Spreadsheets

For many of Excel's basic functions, you have a choice of whether to execute it using the keyboard or the mouse. We provide both, since which you use is a matter of individual preference.

Figure 2.4
The selected cell in the worksheet.

Book1

	A	B	C
1			
2			

Selecting a cell. To enter a value or a label into a cell, you must first select it to make it the focus of keyboard activity. When a cell is selected, a thick black border surrounds it, as shown in Figure 2.4. To select a cell:

- Use the arrow keys on the keyboard to move the focus from one cell to another.

OR

- Move the mouse pointer to a cell and click the primary mouse button.

Selecting a range of cells. You can extend a selection to include a range of cells; the selection border will expand.

- Select the first cell in your range. Hold down the **Shift** key while pressing an arrow key.

OR

- Click on the first cell in your range and hold down the primary mouse button while dragging the mouse pointer over all the cells you wish to highlight.

Moving within a spreadsheet. Note that the spreadsheet is actually much larger than the physical window. To move around within a spreadsheet:

- Use the arrow keys; if you try to move the selection rectangle off the screen to the right or the bottom, the window scrolls.

OR

- Use the mouse and the scroll bars at the right and the bottom of your screen to scroll to your desired position.

Tip: To return to cell A1 at any time, press the **Ctrl** and **Home** keys at the same time.

Entering Data and Correcting Mistakes

Enrollment figures for several sections of Statistics and Experimental Psychology are shown in Figure 2.5. In general, to enter data, simply type the text, value, or formula into the highlighted cell. We realize, however, that what you need to know beyond entering data is how to correct your inevitable mistakes. To practice:

- Select cell A1 of *Sheet 1*.
- Type the word *Sadistics*.
- Press **Enter**; the selected cell is now A2.
- Begin entering the numbers, as shown in Figure 2.5, pressing **Enter** after you have typed each number. (**Enter** lets Excel know you are done entering data in the selected cell and are ready to move down to the next cell.)
- When you finish with column A, move to cell B1; enter data into column B.

Figure 2.5
Example data containing a mistake.

	A	B	C
1	Sadistics	Experimental	
2	25	15	
3	36	21	
4	31	19	
5		17	
6			
7			
8			
9			
10			
11			
12			
13			

Sheet1 / Sheet2 / Sheet3 /

Your spreadsheet should now look like the one in Figure 2.5.

To correct a mistake:

- Select the cell you wish to edit (here, cell A1); the cell contents appear in the **Formula Bar**.

- Click within the contents of the **Formula Bar** to locate the cursor there; a blinking vertical line will appear.
- Edit your entry (here, the word *Sadistics*). Type over existing text, use the arrow keys, the **Delete** key, or the **Back Space** key.
- Press **Enter** when you are finished revising.

Using Formulas

Excel has built-in formulas that allow you to perform common calculations automatically, instead of typing in formulas manually each time you want to perform a common mathematical operation. To access these formulas, use the **Paste Function** icon f_*, which is found on the **Standard Toolbar** (Figure 2.1).

Figure 2.6
Paste Function
dialog box.

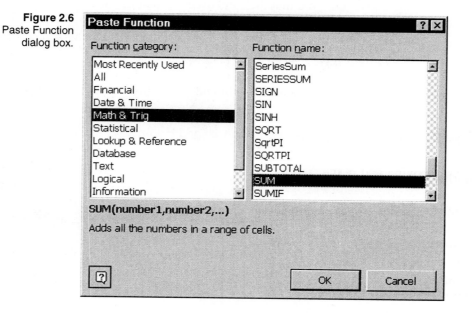

As an exercise, we will use the **SUM** function to get the total enrollment across all the sections of each class.

- Select cell A7 of the class enrollment spreadsheet, using the keyboard or mouse.
- Click on the **Paste Function** icon f_* on the **Standard Toolbar**. **The Paste Function** dialog box will appear, as shown in Figure 2.6.
- Select **Math & Trig** from **Function category**.
- Select **SUM** from **Function name**. Use the scrollbar to reach **SUM**, or, alternatively, with the **Function name** list selected, press the **s** key on the keyboard, which will move you quickly to the names on the list starting with S.
- Click **OK**. As shown in Figure 2.7, the **SUM** dialog box will appear.
- Type in *A2:A4* into the text box labeled **Number 1**. This tells the **SUM** function to compute the sum of cells A2 through A4 and put the result in cell A7.
- Click **OK**, and the formula will be entered into cell A7, which should now be displaying the enrollment total of 92.
- With cell A7 still selected, as shown by the thick border surrounding it, notice that the **SUM** function appears in the **Formula Bar** as =SUM(A2:A4).

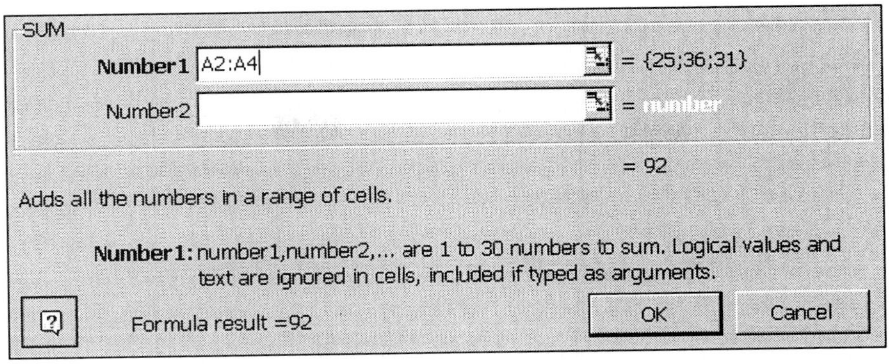

Figure 2.7
SUM dialog box
with cell reference
entered.

Tips:
- As a shortcut, always examine the function names under the **Most Recently Used** category before looking under another category. Functions that you have used recently will appear here.
- Formulas in Excel always start with =.
- When you select a cell that contains a formula, the formula appears in the **Formula Bar** for easy reference or editing.
- You can type formulas directly into a cell by typing = followed by the formula.

Copying and Pasting Functions

Definitions. Copying and moving data or calculations from cell to cell can save a lot of time when you are working with formulas. There are several ways to accomplish copying, pasting, and cutting from cell to cell. First, we should define the terms:
- Copying means to place a replica of a cell or range of cells (value, text, or formula) onto a clipboard (temporary memory storage).
- Cutting means to remove the contents from a cell or range of cells and place it on the clipboard.
- Pasting means to take whatever is on the clipboard and place it into the cell(s) currently selected.

Mouse and Keyboard Techniques. There are many ways to access the copy, cut, and paste commands. Use whichever works best for you.
- Press the secondary mouse button to call up a context menu (see Figure 2.8, left-hand panel).

OR
- Click **Edit** on the **Menu Bar**, and choose **Cut**, **Copy**, or **Paste** there.

OR
- Click on the **Cut** ✂, **Copy** 📋, or **Paste** 📋 icons on the **Standard Toolbar**.

OR
- Use keyboard shortcuts: Press a key simultaneously with the **Ctrl** key. For **Cut**, press **Ctrl-x**; for **Copy**, press **Ctrl-c**; for **Paste**, press **Ctrl-v**.

To perform a cut and paste or copy and paste operation:
- Select a cell or a range of cells.
- Access the **Cut** or **Copy** command using one of the techniques just mentioned.
- Click on the cell where you want the cut or copied cell contents to appear.
- Select **Paste**. The individual cell or entire range of cells should appear.

Example. As an example, let us use the copy function to calculate the enrollment total for the *Experimental* sections. Instead of going through the steps to use **Paste Function** again, we can simply copy the formula from cell A7 to cell B7.

- Use your preferred method to copy cell A7. A blinking, dotted rectangle will appear around cell A7, which tells you that cell is being copied.
- Select cell B7.
- Use your preferred method to paste into cell B7.

Cell B7 will now display 55, which, unfortunately, is not the correct total. To understand why the answer is wrong, highlight cell B7. Examine the formula in the **Formula Bar**: **=SUM(B2:B4)**. Notice that cell B7 is summing cells B2 through B4, and not including the number in cell B5. When we copied the formula from cell A7, Excel adjusted the column references from A to B, but maintained the original cell numbers (2 through 4). Thus, copying the formula did not include the number in Row 5 in the *Experimental* list. The lesson: check your work!

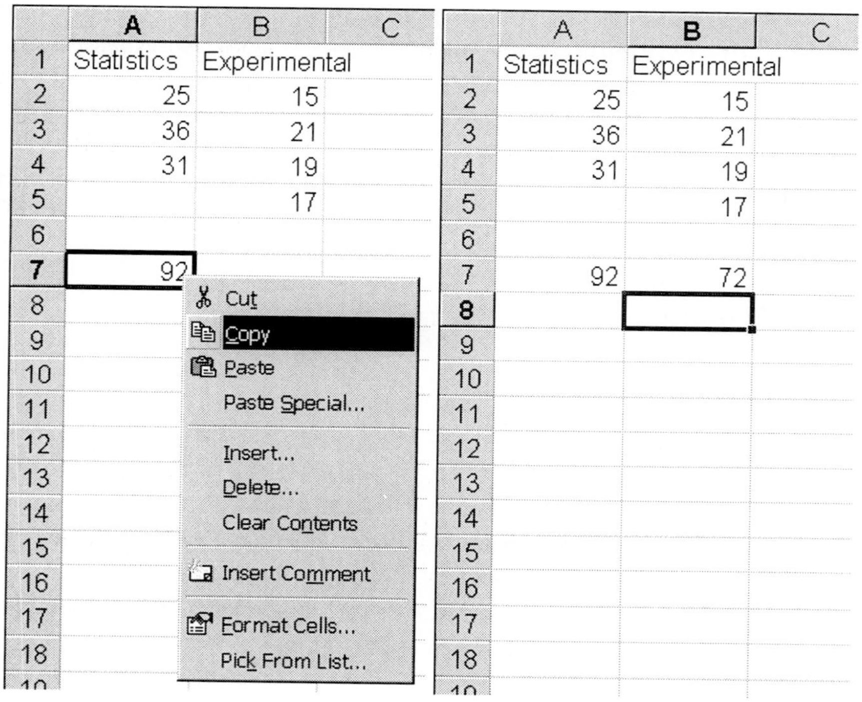

Figure 2.8
Left panel: Choosing Copy from the context menu.

Right panel: The spreadsheet after the copy operation and formula correction.

To correct the formula:

- Click within the contents of the **Formula Bar** to locate the cursor there; a blinking vertical line will appear.
- Edit the numbers so that the formula reads **=SUM(B2:B5)**.
- Press **Enter**. The correct sum, 72, should now appear in cell B7, as shown in the right-hand panel of Figure 2.8.

Undoing and Redoing

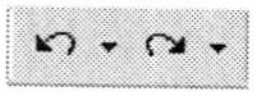

Whenever you make a horrifying mistake with Excel, the damage can usually be undone using the **Undo** command. To execute it:

Figure 2.9
Undo-Redo.

- Choose **Undo** from the **Edit** menu.

OR

- Click the icon on the **Standard Toolbar**, as shown in Figure 2.9; **Undo** is the left-pointing arrow. (If there is nothing to undo, the control will be grayed-out).

OR

- Simultaneously press **Ctrl** and **z** on your keyboard.

You can also **Redo** if you **Undo** and later decide that undoing was a bad idea. Access **Redo** either on the **Standard Toolbar** (the right-pointing arrow in Figure 2.9) or on the **Edit** menu.

Saving and Retrieving Workbooks

Saving. Workbooks can be saved to disk as files; always save your work.

- Choose **File** from the **Menu Bar**.
- Select **Save**. If your file already exists on disk because you have already saved it or you have loaded it from disk, the file will be updated immediately. If the workbook has not yet been saved to disk, a **Save As** dialog box will appear (see Figure 2.10).
- Choose the location where the workbook should be stored. If you are not using your own computer, you will most likely want to store the workbook file on a floppy disk that you can remove from the machine and carry with you. If so, place a formatted floppy disk in the machine and click on the drop-down arrow of **Save in**. A list will appear. Choose **3½ Floppy**, which is usually the **A:** drive. A list of files already on disk will appear in the window. In the **File name** text box, type in the file name. Use *Class Enrollment Data.xls* as the file name for our exercise.
- Click on the **Save** button to complete the action.

Tip: Alternate ways to **Save** are:
- Click on the **Save** icon 🖫 on the **Standard Toolbar** with the mouse.

OR

- Simultaneously press the **Ctrl** and **s** keys on the keyboard.

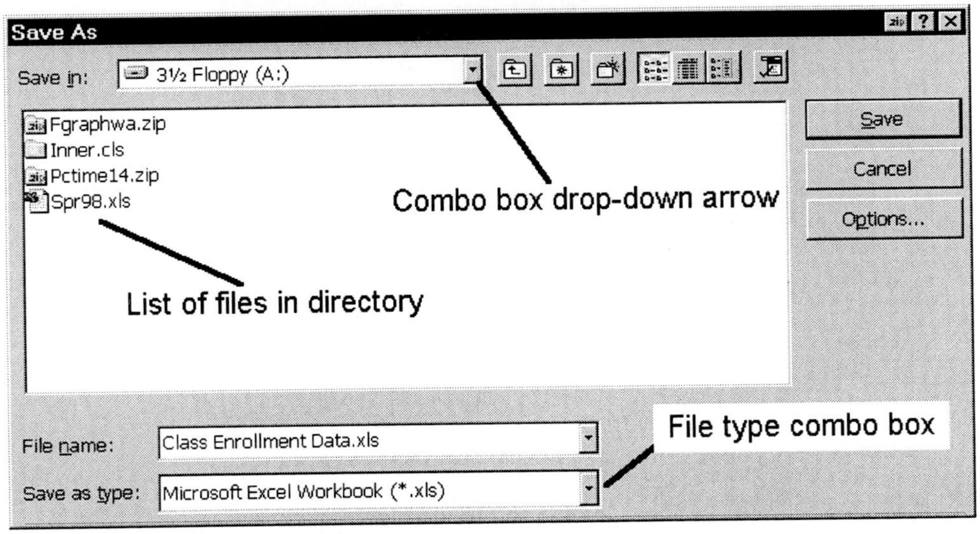

Figure 2.10
Save As dialog box displaying the contents of drive A.

Retrieving. To retrieve a file once it is saved:

- Choose **Open** from the **File** menu. A file **Open** dialog box will appear (see Figure 2.11).
- Locate the drive where you stored the file by clicking the arrow next to **Look in** and selecting the drive from the list.
- Navigate to the correct directory by double-clicking file folder icons ▭ to open file folders and clicking on the up-one-level button ▣ to close them.
- When the desired file name appears in the window, click on it to select it.
- Click on the **Open** button.

Tips:

- To get help on any of the controls, click on the ▣ icon and then click on the control you need help with. **F1** can always provide additional help.

- Alternate ways to retrieve a file:
  - ❖ Click on the **Open** ☞ icon.
  - OR
  - ❖ Simultaneously press the **Ctrl** and **o** keys on the keyboard.

Figure 2.11
Open dialog box.

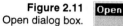

Up one level button

File Folders

Tip: Be aware that you may sometimes encounter earlier versions of Excel. For instance, you may have the Microsoft Office 95 suite at home. Unfortunately, that version of Excel will not be able to read the file created by Excel for Office 97 unless you specifically tell Excel to save the workbook file in the earlier format. To do so, click on the drop-down arrow of **Save as type** and choose the appropriate file type, as shown below. If you are unfamiliar with computers, you may need help choosing the correct file type. If you will always be using the program on the same computer, there is no need to worry about file types—just ignore the **Save as type** box.

Save as type: Microsoft Excel Workbook (*.xls)

Microsoft Excel Workbook (*.xls)
Template (*.xlt)
Formatted Text (Space delimited) (*.prn)
Text (Tab delimited) (*.txt)
Microsoft Excel 5.0/95 Workbook (*.xls)
Microsoft Excel 97 & 5.0/95 Workbook (*.xls)

Printing

There are three main areas of interest related to printing: **Print**, **Print Preview**, and **Page Setup**. You can specify what will be printed, see your work before it is printed, or you can customize the way the printout looks.

Print. Selecting **Print** from the **File** menu produces the **Print** dialog box, which is shown in Figure 2.12. You will most often simply press the **OK** button on this dialog to print the document, but it is possible that you might want to specify a range of pages or print the entire workbook, which are options under **Print what**.

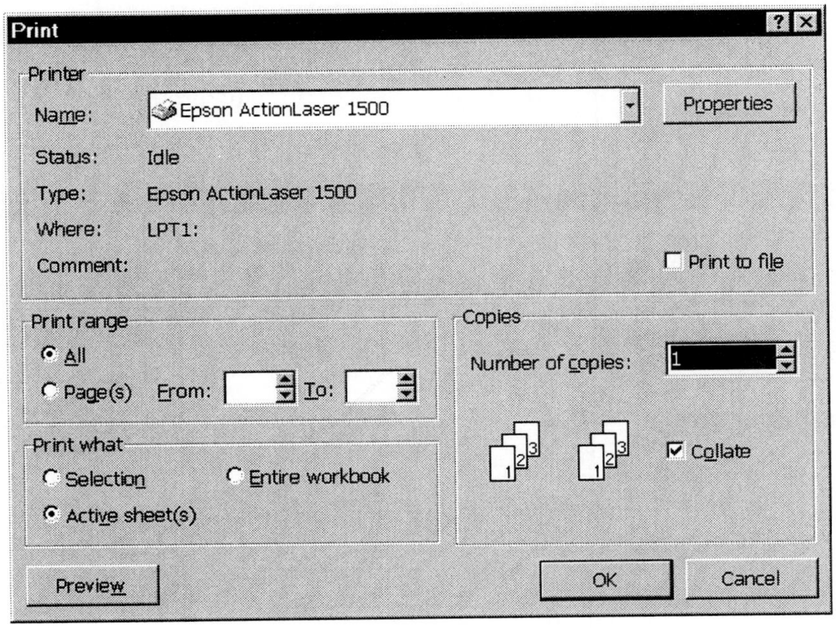

Figure 2.12
Print dialog box.

Print Preview. Selecting **Print Preview** from the **File** menu is an especially good choice, because it gives you an on-screen preview of how the printed page will appear. At the top of the preview screen are a number of buttons (see Figure 2.13) that let you control various aspects of the printed output. For example, the **Zoom** control allows you to magnify small details on the output, and the **Margins** control allows you to set the margins of the page.

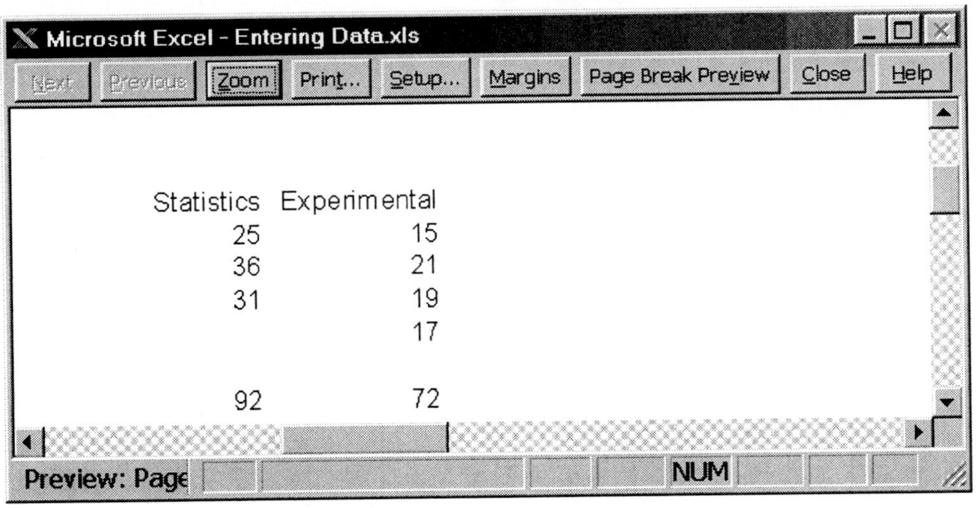

Figure 2.13
Appearance of
the Print Preview
screen.

Clicking on the **Setup** button produces the **Page Setup** dialog box (see Figure 2.14).

Page Setup. This is accessible from the **Print Preview** screen or from the **File** menu. **Page Setup** contains a number of tabbed pages filled with options for customizing your printout.

- **Page.** With this tab you can select **Portrait** versus **Landscape** orientation, which controls whether the printing goes down the page or across the page. You can also control **Scaling**, which allows you to shrink the output to fit on a limited number of pages.
  - **Header/Footer.** You can add headers and/or footers to appear on your printout. These help you identify the contents of your work.
  - **Sheet.** Checking **Gridlines** under **Print** will produce gridlines on the printed page that match those found on the computer screen.

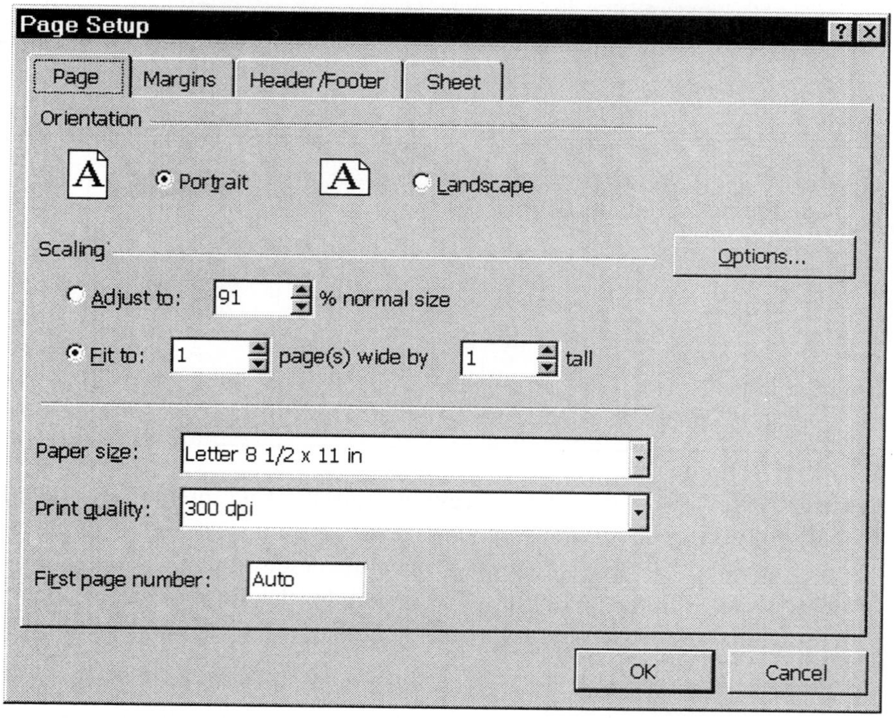

Figure 2.14
Page Setup
dialog box.

Tip: Print area allows you to print only a portion of a spreadsheet. For example, entering the range A1:B7 into this **Page Setup** control tells Excel to print only cells in the block formed by A1 in the upper left hand corner, and B7 in the lower right hand corner.

    ✓ *Important!* Choose **Page Setup** from the **File** menu if you wish to alter the print area. If you access the **Page Setup** dialog box from **Print Preview**, the control will be grayed-out and unusable.

Instead of manually typing a cell range, the print area can also be set by highlighting a range of cells on the spreadsheet, selecting **Print Area** from the **File** menu, and then clicking on **Set Print Area**.

Step-by-Step Practice Exercise

1. Open a new Excel spreadsheet and in Column A enter a variable label and 5 data cases. Insert a disk and save the file to a 3½ floppy drive using the name *Practice*.

2. Close the *Practice* file.

3. Open a new Excel spreadsheet (**New** command in the **File** menu) and in Column A enter a variable label and 5 data cases.

4. Save the file to a folder on your C: drive using the name *Junkdata*. Do not close the file.

5. Retrieve the *Practice* file. (If you are having trouble finding it, remember that you should be looking for the file on the 3½ floppy drive, not your local C: drive).

6. Once you have the *Practice* file open, highlight the contents of the *Junkdata* file and copy them to column B of the *Practice* file.

7. Save the new contents of *Practice*.

Frequency Distributions and Histograms

Overview

In this module, we will create a grouped frequency distribution table and a histogram through the **Analysis ToolPak** procedure, **Histogram**, which works well if you are starting with raw data. If you have already created a frequency distribution table, however, the **Chart Wizard** is the best way to go (see *Chapter 4, Bar and Line Charts*).

The creation of grouped frequency distributions and histograms are both endeavors requiring some forethought. To illustrate the process, we will use the following example:

A human factors psychologist was asked to aid in the design of an automated information kiosk for a large shopping mall. As one test of the kiosk's user interface, 25 subjects queried the system for the location of a particular shop in the mall. The psychologist recorded the time in seconds for each subject to make the query. Of the 25 subjects, 24 completed the query successfully. Figure 3.1 shows the times already input into an Excel spreadsheet.

Reproduce the data in your own spreadsheet by typing the label *Observations* in cell A1 and then typing in the data below the label. Next, we need to decide on three characteristics for our distribution.

Figure 3.1
Data from the kiosk study.

	A
1	Observations
2	67.5
3	52.8
4	75.7
5	91.1
6	89.9
7	98.0
8	39.2
9	68.5
10	88.4
11	55.7
12	61.6
13	46.6
14	44.3
15	57.3
16	60.4
17	40.2
18	63.5
19	65.9
20	74.0
21	66.5
22	67.1
23	66.4
24	78.1
25	70.7

How Many Class Intervals Should Be Used?

Different sources suggest different answers to this simple question. Some suggest that we should aim for 6-10 groupings or class intervals, while others suggest 10-20 intervals. Probably the best answer is to say that we should choose a number that neither hides too much information nor presents too much information. Setting too many intervals produces a table that is long, cumbersome, and poor at summarizing the data; setting too few produces a table that fails to summarize because it loses too much important detail.

A good starting place is to consider the range and number of scores in the distribution. To find the range of our set of scores, we could use Excel's **MIN** and **MAX** functions (see *Chapter 2, Spreadsheet Basics,* for instructions on using Excel's **Paste Function** commands), or we could use the **Analysis ToolPak's Descriptive Statistics** tool (see *Chapter 5, Descriptive Statistics*). Another method is to sort the data from lowest to highest.

- Highlight the range of cells from A1 to A25 using the mouse or the keyboard.
- Click the **Sort Ascending** icon ⬇ on the **Standard Toolbar**.

Scrolling through the sorted times, we can see that the shortest time to make a query was 39.2 seconds and the longest time was 98 seconds. With a range of about 59 (range = maximum - minimum score) and 24 data points to fit in, it makes little sense to have a large number of class intervals – six to eight should work just fine.

What Size Should Each Class Interval Be?

Several constraints apply to this question:
- All the intervals should be the same width.
- The entire range of scores must be covered without gaps or overlaps.
- The bottom score in each class interval should be a multiple of the interval width. For example, if we were to choose an interval of five and the lowest score were 39.2, we should have class intervals starting at 35, 40, 45, and so on.
- The interval width should generally be something that is easy for readers to count by. For instance, 1, 2, 5, 10, 20, 50, and 100 are numbers that most people find easy to mentally add and subtract.
- The interval should reflect the conventions of the research area and make common sense.

For our example, an interval width of 10 can be comprehended easily, and the entire range of observed times can be covered in seven intervals.

What Should the Lower and Upper Real Limits Be?

With an interval size of 10, the apparent limits of our class intervals will be 30-39, 40-49, and so on. The actual range of scores contained within the first class interval will be 29.5-39.5 (actually, $29.5 - 39.4\overline{9}$). The number 29.5 is the lower real limit (LRL) of the interval, and 39.5 ($39.4\overline{9}$) is the upper real limit (URL).

- Enter the column heading for the URLs in cell B1. This will be used for the X-axis label of the histogram.
- Enter the URLs for the class intervals from lowest to highest in cells B2 through B8, as shown in Figure 3.2.

Figure 3.2
Kiosk data with URLs in column B.

	A	B
1	Observations	Query Times (seconds)
2	67.5	39.49
3	52.8	49.49
4	75.7	59.49
5	91.1	69.49
6	89.9	79.49
7	98.0	89.49
8	39.2	99.49

Note: Frequency distribution tables in the behavioral sciences are usually arranged in descending order. Excel's **Histogram** procedure will only work correctly if the URLs are arranged in ascending order.

Note that the number of decimal places in each URL should be one greater than the number of decimal places in the data. For instance, if your data maintain two decimal places of precision instead of one, use three decimal places for the URLs in column B (e.g, 39.499, 49.499, etc.).

Creating the Frequency Distribution Table and Histogram

Step 1: Choose the Analysis Procedure

- Click on **Tools** and a menu drops down, as shown on the left in Figure 3.3.
- Click on **Data Analysis** and a menu drops down, as shown on the right in Figure 3.3.
- Scroll downward to highlight **Histogram**.
- Click on the **OK** button.

Figure 3.3
Tools menu and the Data Analysis dialog box.

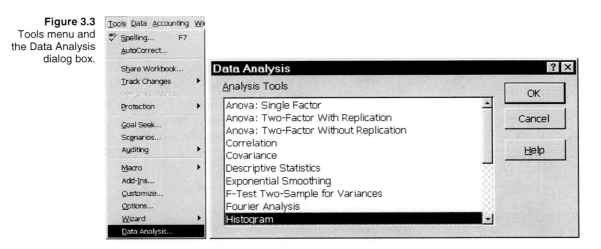

Step 2: Fill in the Dialog Box

Complete the dialog box as shown in Figure 3.4, then click the **OK** button to perform the analysis.

Figure 3.4
Histogram dialog box.

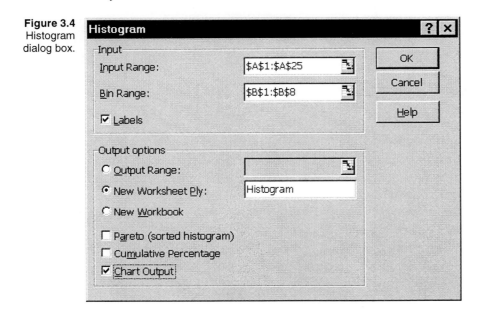

Input Range. Enter the cell locations of the data (**A1:A25**), including the variable label. If you choose to highlight the spreadsheet cells instead of manually typing in the cell range here, Excel adds the dollar signs seen in Figure 3.4.

Bin Range. Enter the cell locations of the URLs of our intervals (**B1:B8**), including the label.

Labels. Be sure to check this box so that the label *Query Times (seconds)* will appear on the frequency distribution table and the histogram. When your input range includes the cell with your variable name, you must check this box or else Excel will give an error message.

Output Options. Excel provides three choices for the output's location:
- **Output Range** places the output on the same spreadsheet page as your original data; you specify the cell location for the upper left corner of the output, e.g. cell D1.
- **New Worksheet Ply** is the default output location. Excel pastes the output into a new worksheet in the current workbook. Your data and output are kept together in the same file. You have the option to name the new worksheet by typing a name into the text box. If you do not name the new sheet, Excel will name it *Sheet 4,* or the next available name in the series (*Sheets 1, 2,* and *3* are created whenever you start a new Excel workbook). For our exercise, name the new sheet *Histogram.*
- **New Workbook** means Excel pastes the output into a different workbook from the one containing the data. This is probably the least desirable option, as your data and statistical analyses will not be together in the same Excel file.

Tip: When Excel pastes output into a spreadsheet, labels and values in the output may be cut off, because the columns are not wide enough. To widen a column, position the mouse pointer over the divider to the right of the column. When the pointer changes to a cross ✛, hold down the primary mouse button and drag the column's edge to the right. Release the mouse button when everything is visible.

Pareto (sorted histogram). This option will produce a second frequency distribution table sorted by *Frequency*. We will not use this option for our exercise.

Cumulative Percentage. This option will produce a *Cumulative Percent* column in the frequency distribution table. It will also add a *Cumulative Percent* data series to the histogram, if the **Chart Output** option is chosen. Again, we will not use this option.

Chart Output. Check this option to produce a histogram. Otherwise, only a frequency distribution table will be produced.

Step 3: Interpret the Results of the Procedure

After completing Step 2 and widening columns, you should have output that looks like Figure 3.5. A frequency distribution table is on the left and a histogram is on the right. The procedure copied our URL column (*Query Times*) to the new worksheet and added one column and one row. The *Frequency* column is simply the count of scores observed within each class interval. The *More* row is a class that Excel adds to catch any scores above the highest URL.

Figure 3.5
Initial output of the Histogram procedure.

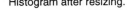

	A	B	C	D	E	F	G	H	I
1	Query Times (seconds)	Frequency							
2	39.49	1							
3	49.49	3							
4	59.49	3							
5	69.49	9							
6	79.49	4							
7	89.49	1							
8	99.49	3							
9	More	0							
10									

Finishing the Histogram

Excel's default chart is not yet a true histogram. In the steps that follow, we will produce an acceptable histogram that is also presentation quality.

Resize the Histogram

You want to see all the values and labels on the X- and Y-axes.
- Click anywhere in the white area surrounding the chart. Eight little square *handles* should appear, as shown in Figure 3.6.
- Place the mouse pointer over one of the handles so that the pointer changes to a resizing arrow (↕, ↗, or ↘). Hold the primary mouse button down and drag until the histogram is completely visible. (Selecting one of the corner handles will allow you to resize both the vertical and horizontal axes simultaneously).

After resizing, the histogram should look something like the one in Figure 3.6.

Figure 3.6
Histogram after resizing.

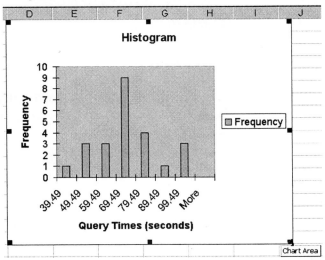

Revise the X-Axis Values

Excel inserts the URLs as labels for the X-axis. Histograms typically use either the apparent limits or the midpoint of each interval as axis labels. We will use the apparent limits.

The easiest way to change the labels along the X-axis is to change them in column A of the frequency distribution table Excel generated as part of the **Histogram** procedure.

- Replace cells A2 through A8 with the labels shown in Figure 3.7.

Delete the *More* Row

Unless you have an open-ended frequency distribution, the *More* category will be empty and should be deleted.

Figure 3.7
Bringing up the context menu after changing the labels of Column A.

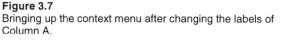

	A	B	C
1	Query Times (seconds)	Frequency	
2	30-39	1	
3	40-49	3	
4	50-59	3	
5	60-69	9	
6	70-79	4	
7	80-89	1	
8	90-99	3	
9	More		
10			
11			
12			
13			
14			
15			
16			
17			
18			
19			
20			
21			

Context menu:
- Cut
- Copy
- Paste
- Paste Special...
- Insert...
- Delete...
- Clear Contents
- Insert Comment
- Format Cells...
- Pick From List...

- Select the row labeled *More*, which is in cells A9 through B9.
- Center the mouse pointer vertically in the selected range and click the secondary mouse button. A context menu should appear, as shown in Figure 3.7.
- Select **Delete** from the menu.
- When the dialog box appears select **Shift cells up** and click **OK**.

> **Tip: Shift cells up** tells Excel to move all the cells below A9:B9 up to fill the space vacated by cells A9:B9. Pressing the **Delete** key would not have had the same effect as selecting **Delete** from the context menu. Pressing the **Delete** key clears the contents of the highlighted cells, but does not remove the *More* category from the histogram.

Delete the Legend

Since we do not need the legend, delete it to give the histogram more room.
- Click anywhere on the legend and eight little square handles will appear around it.
- Press the **Delete** key.

Add a Functional Title

We need to edit the title to make it more descriptive.
- Click on the current title, *Histogram*, so that selection handles appear around it.
- Click once on the text inside the box and a blinking vertical edit cursor should appear.
- Replace the title *Histogram* with *Distribution of Times Required to Query for the Location of a Shop.*

Widen the Bars to Span the Class Interval

On a proper histogram, the bars touch and each bar on the chart spans its entire class interval. We need to make this bar chart look like a histogram.

- Click on one of the bars. Selection handles will appear on all the bars in the series.
- Click the secondary mouse button to bring up the context menu shown in Figure 3.8.
- Select **Format Data Series**.
- Select the **Options** tab (see Figure 3.9).
- Change **Gap width** to zero.
- Click on **OK** and the spaces between the bars on the chart will disappear.

Figure 3.8
Effect of clicking on the data series.

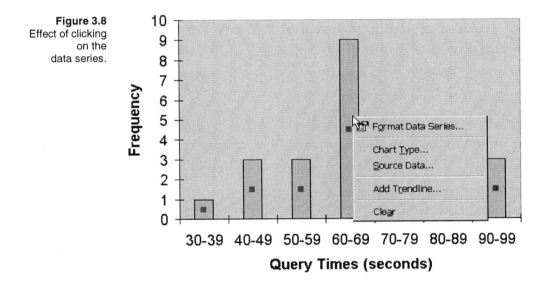

Figure 3.9
The Format Data Series dialog box.

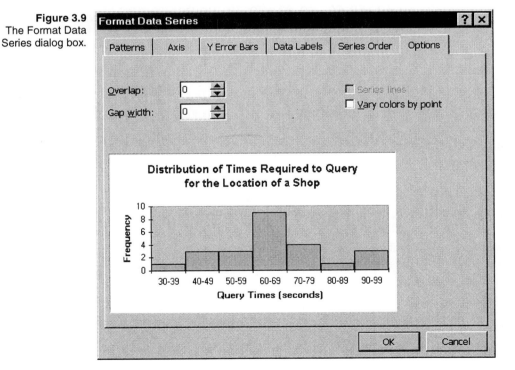

Change the Background to White

As a final customization, change the background color to white so that the image will reproduce better on black and white printers.

- Double-click anywhere in the gray plot area around the bars, and the dialog box titled **Format Plot Area** will appear.
- Under **Area**, pick white from the color grid and click **OK**.

The final histogram should resemble the one in Figure 3.10.

Figure 3.10
The completed
histogram.

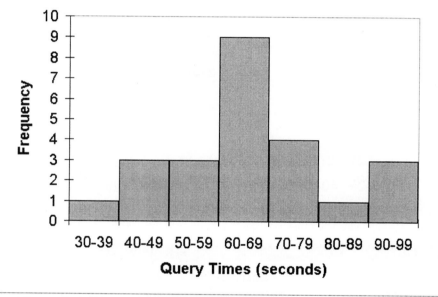

Distribution of Times Required to Query for the Location of a Shop

Step-by-Step Practice Exercise

1. Make up 25-30 observations similar to those in this chapter, but use a different range of scores. Insert an appropriate column of URLs next to the data you made up. Be sure that your intervals cover the entire range of scores, are equally sized, and leave no gaps in the distribution.

2. Use the **Histogram** tool to produce a grouped frequency distribution table and histogram. Place the results on a separate sheet named *Histogram*.

3. Replace the URL labels in the frequency distribution table with the apparent limits of each interval. Delete the *More* category if is empty. If *More* is not empty, you have an error in your URLs. Correct your URLs, then repeat Steps 2 and 3.

4. Adjust the appearance of the histogram by resizing it, deleting the legend, and adding a more functional title.

5. Save your file using the name *Histogram*.

Bar and Line Charts

There are many useful chart types to help with the visualization and comprehension of data. In Chapter 3, we described how to construct histograms to display frequency data. Here, we will illustrate how to construct presentation-quality bar charts and line charts. These charts can be used to display a variety of data types such as frequency, percentages, and average scores.

Creating a Bar Chart

Bar charts are generally preferred when the variable plotted on the X-axis is categorical rather than quantitative. The arbitrary ordering of the categories is conveyed visually by the appearance of discrete bars separated by empty spaces. Making a bar chart is a fairly simple task using the **Chart Wizard**. Just bear in mind that Excel calls charts containing vertical bars, *column charts,* and charts containing horizontal bars, *bar charts*. Although both types are used with categorical data, bars in the vertical orientation are what we see most often see in textbooks and the popular press. In the parlance of Excel, we are going to create a column chart to display our data.

To begin, type in the category names and frequency counts presented in Figure 4.1. These data were the counts of different kinds of animals observed on a nature walk. Next, highlight all the data, including the column labels (cells A1:C2).

Figure 4.1
Sample data for creating a bar chart.

	A	B	C
1	Reptiles	Mammals	Birds
2	22	11	36
3			

Chart Wizard Step 1: Chart Type

After highlighting your data, activate **Chart Wizard** by clicking the icon on the **Standard Toolbar** located beneath the menu bar. The **Chart Wizard** displays the first of four dialog boxes. Here you select the type of chart you wish to create (see Figure 4.2).
- Choose **Column** under **Chart Type**.
- Accept the default column chart chosen by Excel under **Chart sub-type**.
- Click and hold the **Press and hold to view sample** button to get a chart preview.
- Click on **Next** to bring up Step 2.

Figure 4.2
Chart Wizard
Step 1.

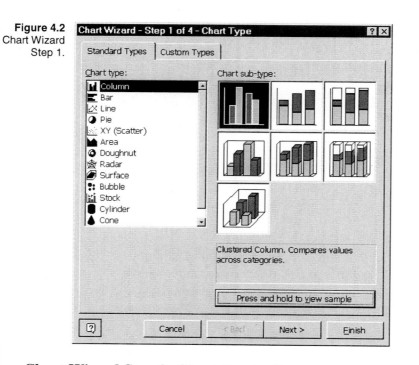

Chart Wizard Step 2: Chart Source Data

If you highlighted the proper cell range before calling up the **Chart Wizard**, your chart will appear correctly and you may move on to Step 3 by clicking the **Next** button.

As a point of interest, however, let's examine the two tabs of the Step 2 dialog box. As can be seen in Figure 4.3, you can specify whether the data series is in the rows or the columns. Our numbers extend along row 2, so the **Chart Wizard** made a correct decision. The **Data range** for producing the chart is the one we selected before starting **Chart Wizard**. If you select the correct range initially, you should never have to adjust this control.

The **Series** tab (see Figure 4.4) provides a more detailed view

Figure 4.3
Chart Wizard Step 2 (Data Range tab visible).

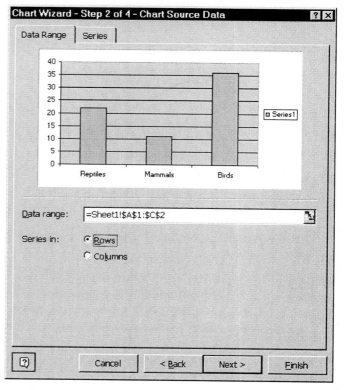

of how the data range is being used. The **Values** box contains the range of spreadsheet cells that are being plotted as bars. The **Category (X) axis labels** box contains the range of cells that are being used as labels along the X-axis. If you ever do need to adjust any ranges, do not type them into the box directly. Direct typing works for most dialog boxes in Excel, but not for the **Chart Wizard**. Instead, click in the box containing the range you wish to adjust, delete everything there, and highlight the new range on the spreadsheet using the mouse.

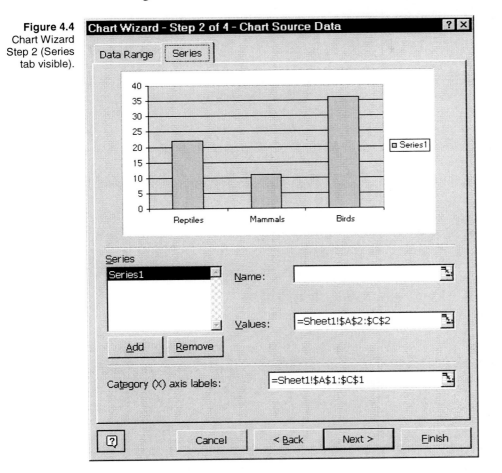

Figure 4.4
Chart Wizard
Step 2 (Series
tab visible).

Chart Wizard Step 3: Chart Options

The third step of the **Chart Wizard**, shown in Figure 4.5, presents several tab sheets of options for formatting the chart. You at least need to add titles and revise the legend.

- On the **Titles** sheet, enter *Counts of three different classes of animals observed on a nature walk* as the chart title.
- For the X-axis title, enter *Class of Animal*, and for the Y-axis title enter *Count*.
- To delete the legend, click on the **Legend** tab and uncheck the **Show legend** box. The default legend label Excel uses, *Series 1,* will disappear. (With only one variable it makes no sense to include a legend. Conversely, a legend would be necessary if the data had been categorized along two dimensions (for example, by endangered vs. non-endangered species *and* by class of animal).
- Explore the other tabs and options available, such as turning off gridlines. When you are finished customizing the chart, click **Next** to move on to Step 4.

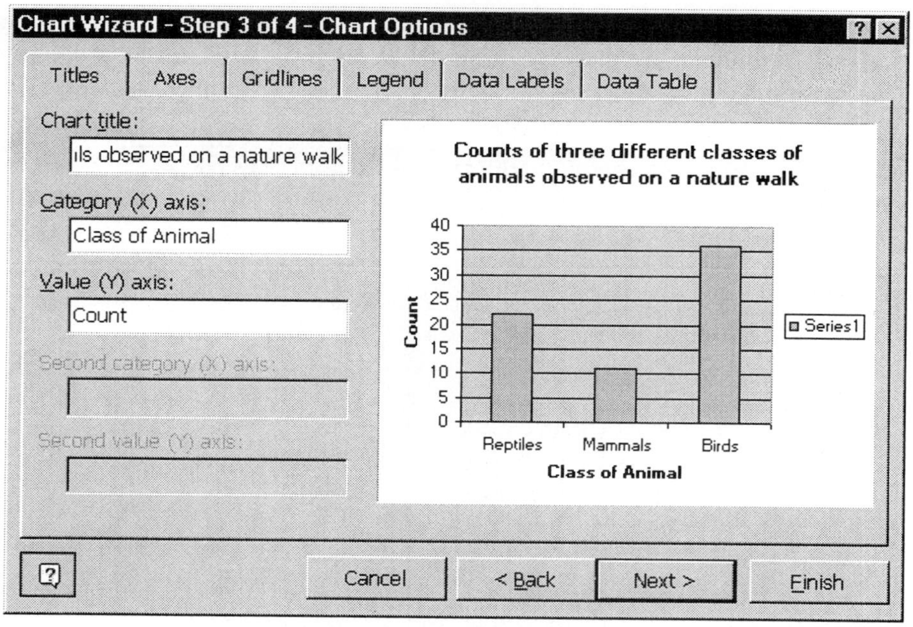

Figure 4.5
Chart Wizard
Step 3.

Chart Wizard Step 4: Chart Location

This step allows you to select the destination of the chart (see Figure 4.6). The default option is to place the chart in the current sheet as a chart object, meaning that the chart will appear alongside the data on the same page. For this exercise, we will place the chart on a new sheet by itself.

- Click the **As new sheet** button.
- Type in a title. For our exercise use *Nature Walk*.
- Click **Finish** and the chart will appear on a fresh sheet.

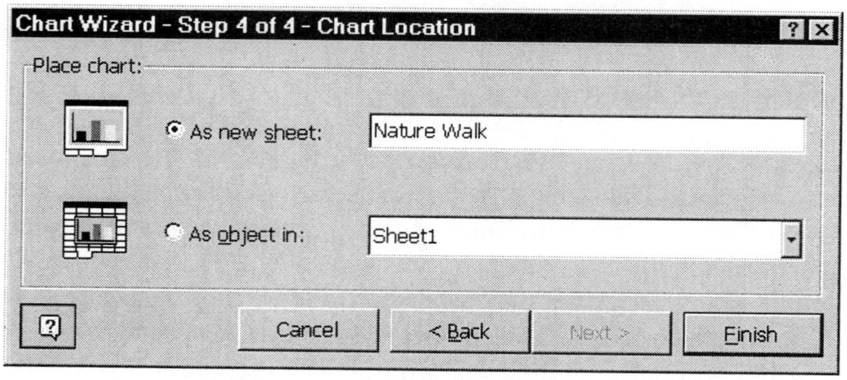

Figure 4.6
Chart Wizard
Step 4.

Finishing the Bar Chart

Once you have generated the chart, you can customize it in many different ways to make it presentation-quality. Clicking on any chart element with the secondary mouse button brings up a context menu of formatting choices; alternatively, you can double-click on the chart element. Apply these finishing touches so that your chart looks similar to the one in Figure 4.9:

- Change the gray background in the plot area to white so that the chart will show up better on black and white printers. Double-click anywhere within the gray area. A dialog box labeled **Format Plot Area** should appear, as shown in Figure 4.7. Click on the white color square and then click **OK**.

- Adjust font sizes because the labels look small. Double-click on either the X-axis or any of the X-axis labels (*Reptiles, Mammals,* or *Birds*). The **Format Axis** dialog box will appear. Choose the **Font** tab, as demonstrated in Figure 4.8, and change the **Size** to at least 14. Click **OK**. Resize the font sizes of the Y-axis and all other labels and titles by double-clicking them.

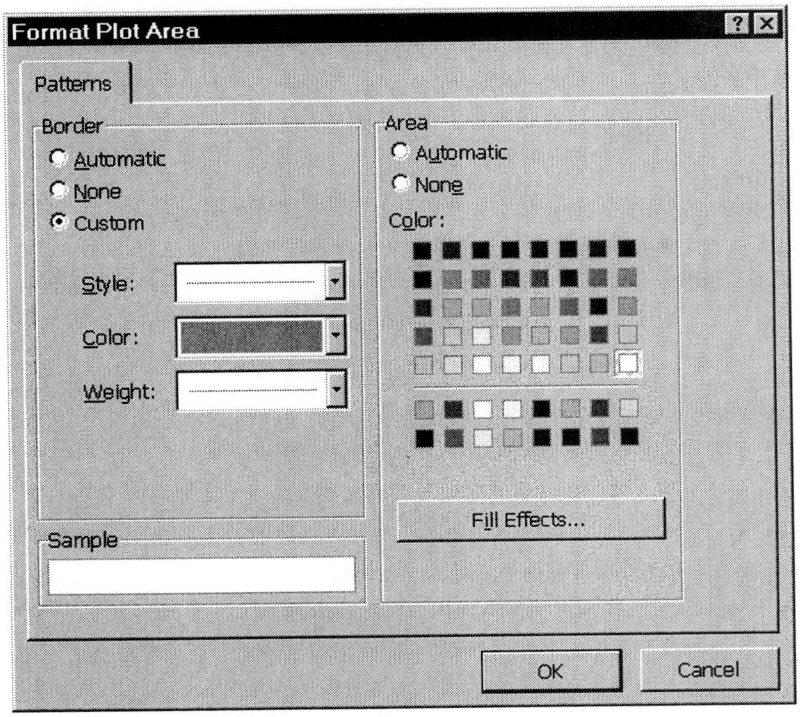

Figure 4.7
Format Plot Area
dialog box.

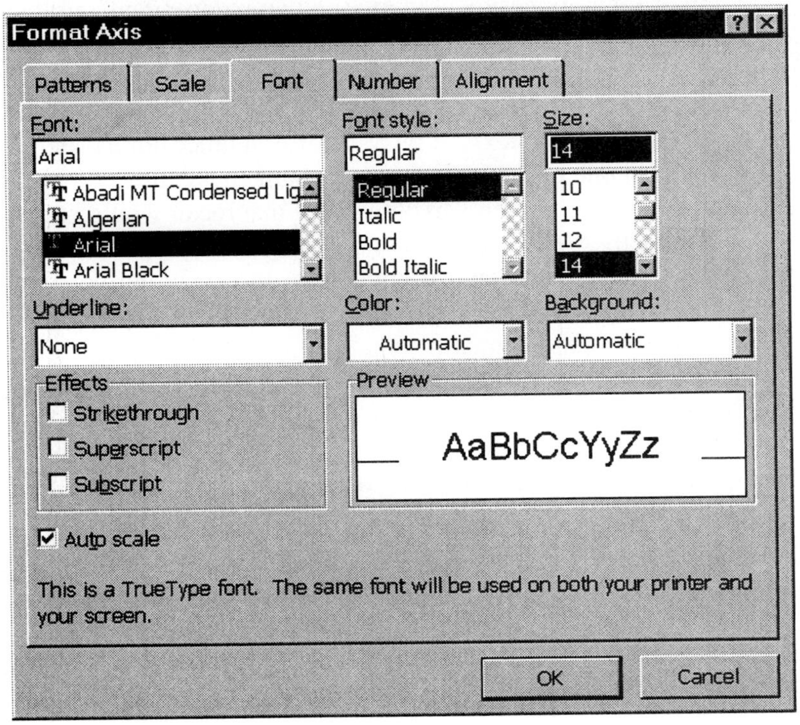

Figure 4.8
Format Axis
dialog box.

Figure 4.9
Completed bar
chart.

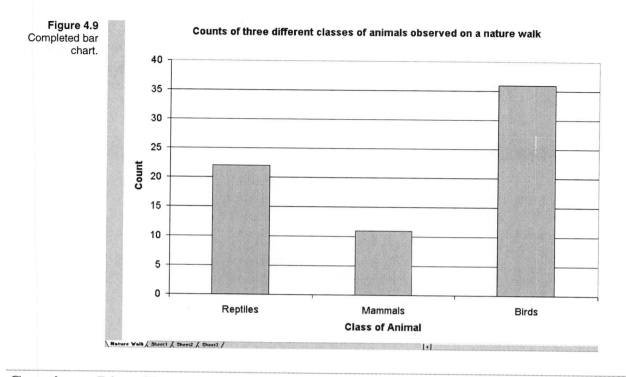

Creating a Line Chart

Line charts are preferred if the independent variable is continuous and ordered, and the dependent variable varies as a function of the value of the independent variable. They can also be used as an alternative to a histogram for depicting frequency information. Finally, line charts may be used to display the results of experiments, especially if a bar chart would be visually crowded or confusing. In our example, we will use a line chart to show the results of this memory experiment involving two independent variables:

Students in an experimental psychology course examined the effects of physical context on recall of word lists. Participants in the experiment encoded a list of words in one of two physical contexts: a busy diner or a quiet library. Four hours later, they recalled the list in one of three contexts: the same busy diner, a bookstore café, or the same quiet library. The students hypothesized that recall would be best if the retrieval context was exactly the same as the encoding context, and would be worst if the retrieval context was completely different from the encoding context. They proposed that recall accuracy would be intermediate if the recall context was similar, but not identical to, the encoding context.

Begin by entering the average (mean) percentage of words recalled for each group into cells A1 through D3, as shown in Figure 4.10. When you have entered all the data, highlight the range A1 through D3 by dragging the cursor.

Figure 4.10
Memory
experiment data.

	A	B	C	D
1		Diner	Café	Library
2	Encode in Diner	66	59	41
3	Encode in Library	35	55	60

Chart Wizard Step 1: Chart Type

After highlighting your data, activate **Chart Wizard** by clicking the icon 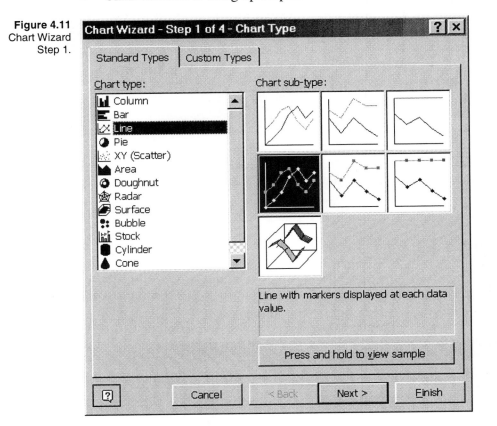 on the **Standard Toolbar** located beneath the menu bar. The **Chart Wizard** displays the first of four dialog boxes. Here you select the type of chart you wish to create (see Figure 4.11).
- Choose **Line** under **Chart type**.
- Use the default line graph under **Chart sub-type**.
- Click and hold the **Press and hold to view sample** button to get a chart preview.
- Click on **Next** to bring up Step 2.

Figure 4.11
Chart Wizard
Step 1.

Chart Wizard Step 2: Chart Source Data

When the **Step 2 of 4** screen comes up, make sure you have selected the correct data range. If so, click **Next**. If not, refer back to *Creating Bar Charts: Chart Wizard Step 2* for further information on this step.

Chart Wizard Step 3: Chart Options

The third step (see Figure 4.12) presents several tab sheets of options for formatting the chart. Perform the following actions so the chart will have a polished appearance:
- Replace the default chart title with *Percent Recall as a Function of Retrieval Context*.
- Enter the title for the X-axis: *Retrieval Context*.
- Enter the title for the Y-axis: *Percent Recall*.

- Choose the **Gridlines** tab. Turn off the gridlines by unchecking **Major gridlines** under **Value (Y) axis**.
- Click **Next**.

Figure 4.12
Chart Wizard
Step 2.

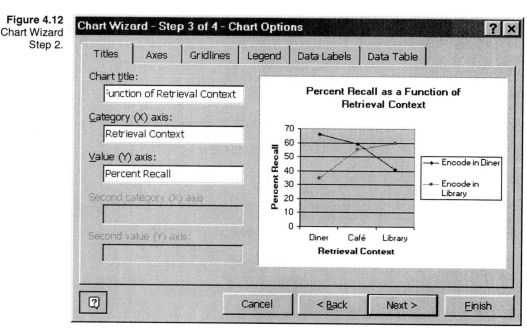

Figure 4.12
Chart Wizard
Step 2.

Chart Wizard Step 4: Chart Location

As seen in Figure 4.13, in step 4 you choose whether to locate the chart on a new sheet or place it as an object in the current sheet. For our exercise, click **Finish** to accept the default option of placing the chart in the current sheet.

Figure 4.13
Chart Wizard
Step 4.

Finishing the Line Chart

- Click on the chart to select it for resizing. Expand the chart by dragging one of the handles of the chart's selection box with the mouse.
- Remove the gray background so the chart will show up better on black and white printers. Position the pointer within the gray plot area and click the secondary mouse button. When the context menu appears, choose **Format Plot Area** and from its dialog box (see Figure 4.7) choose **None** under **Area**.

- Double-click on each data line on the graph to bring up the **Format Data Series** dialog box shown in Figure 4.14. Here you can modify the marker symbol, size, color, and the line style and color. Increase the symbol size to 8, and make the markers and lines black to show up better on black and white printers.
- Increase the size of labels and titles to size 14 or larger. Refer back to *Creating Bar Charts* and Figure 4.8. For help with other customizations, consult Excel's Help files.

Figure 4.14
Format Data
Series dialog box.

The finished graph should look like the one in Figure 4.15. It shows that the psychology students' hypothesis was supported: Recall accuracy is best when study location matches retrieval location. This is a well-known principle applied when "re-enacting the scene of the crime" to jog a person's memory. Perhaps students could take a lesson from this and study in the classrooms where tests are administered rather than studying elsewhere!

Figure 4.15
The finished line
chart.

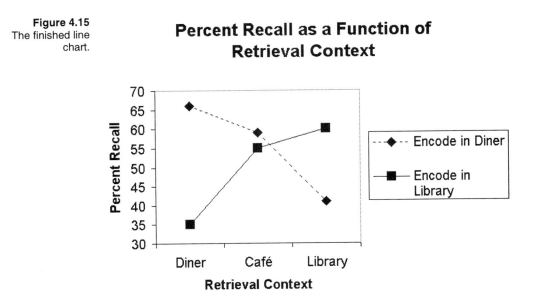

Step-by-Step Practice Exercise

1. On *Sheet 1,* make up data comparing the frequency counts of three categories.

2. Use **Chart Wizard** to create a bar (column) chart.

3. Label your X- and Y-axes, add a title, delete the legend, and adjust font sizes.

4. Place your chart on a separate sheet from the spreadsheet data. Name the sheet *Bar chart.*

5. On *Sheet 2,* make up data for a study consisting of two independent variables. Choose a reasonable dependent variable, but make it something other than recall percentage. Near your data, type a brief description of your hypothetical study.

6. Use **Chart Wizard** to create a line chart.

7. Label your X- and Y-axes, give your chart a descriptive title, and adjust font sizes.

8. Place your chart on the same sheet as the spreadsheet data.

9. Make any other stylistic touches desired for each chart.

10. Save your file using the name *Charts.*

Descriptive Statistics

Descriptive statistics primarily include measures of central tendency (mean, median, mode) and measures of variability (range, standard deviation, variance). The easiest way to find descriptive statistics on a data set is to use Excel's **Analysis ToolPak**, because it provides output on a wide variety of statistics using just one procedure. Excel's built-in **Paste Function** can compute a wider variety of descriptive statistics, including those that are not produced by the **Analysis ToolPak's Descriptive Statistics** procedure. However, **Paste Function's** flexibility comes at the sacrifice of convenience, as statistics must be computed using individual commands.

Descriptive Statistics Using the Analysis ToolPak

Step 1: Enter the Data

Figure 5.1
Data on television watching.

As an example, imagine that we have gathered data on the television watching habits of 11 subjects. Each subject provided an estimate of how many hours per week he or she spends watching television. Enter the resulting data in a spreadsheet, as shown in Figure 5.1.

	A
	Book2
1	TV Hours
2	10
3	14
4	16
5	8
6	20
7	10
8	14
9	15
10	6
11	14
12	12

Step 2: Choose the Analysis

- From the **Tools** menu choose **Data Analysis**.
- Scroll down and highlight **Descriptive Statistics** in the **Data Analysis** dialog box (see Figure 5.2).
- Click on the **OK** button.

Figure 5.2
Data Analysis
dialog box.

Data Analysis ? ✕

Analysis Tools

OK

Anova: Single Factor
Anova: Two-Factor With Replication
Anova: Two-Factor Without Replication
Correlation
Covariance
Descriptive Statistics
Exponential Smoothing
F-Test Two-Sample for Variances
Fourier Analysis
Histogram

Cancel

Help

Step 3: Fill in the Dialog Box

Complete the dialog box shown in Figure 5.3, and then click the **OK** button to run the analysis. Do not change any of Excel's default options without a specific reason when analyzing your own data.

Figure 5.3
Descriptive
Statistics dialog
box.

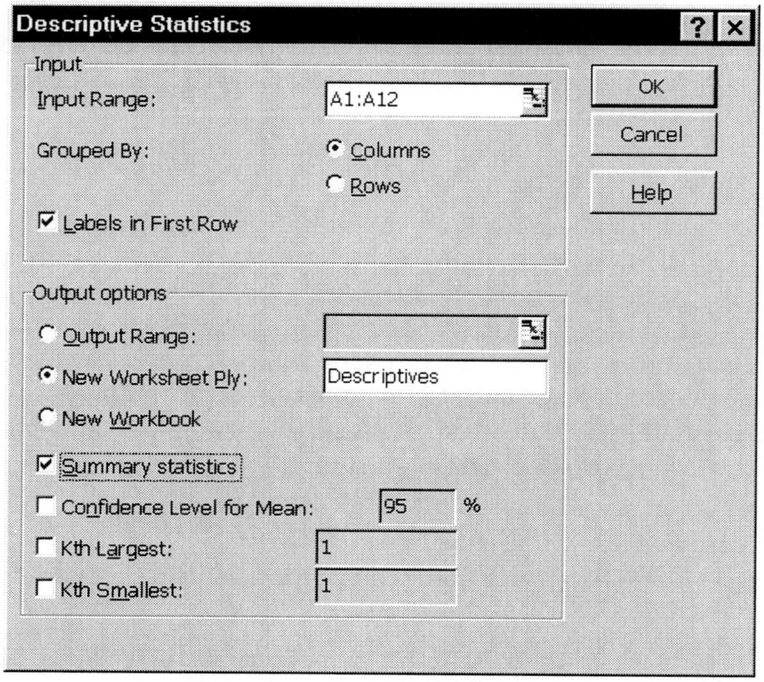

Descriptive Statistics	? ✕

Input

Input Range: `A1:A12`

Grouped By: ● Columns
              ○ Rows

☑ Labels in First Row

OK
Cancel
Help

Output options

○ Output Range:

● New Worksheet Ply: `Descriptives`

○ New Workbook

☑ Summary statistics

☐ Confidence Level for Mean: `95`   %

☐ Kth Largest: `1`

☐ Kth Smallest: `1`

Input Range. Enter the spreadsheet cell location of the data for which you wish to find descriptive statistics. In the TV example, the data, including the variable name, are located in cells A1:A12.

Grouped By. Indicate whether your data variable is found down a column or across a row. Data entry in Excel is typically in column format so this is already marked as the default option.

Labels in First Row. You have the option of adding a variable label to your statistical output and you should always check this box. Labels serve as a clear reminder of what the summary statistics relate to (here, TV hours watched). If your input range included the cell with your variable name, you must check this box or else Excel will give an error message.

Output Options. Excel provides three choices for the output's location:
- **Output** Range places the output on the same spreadsheet page as your original data; you specify the cell location for the upper left corner of the output, e.g. cell D1.
- **New Worksheet Ply** is the default output location. Excel pastes the output into a new worksheet in the current workbook. Your data and output are kept together in the same file. You have the option to name the new worksheet by typing a name into the text box. If you do not name the new sheet, Excel will name it *Sheet 4,* or the next available name in the series (*Sheets 1, 2,* and *3* are created whenever you start a new Excel workbook). For our exercise, name the new sheet *Descriptives.*

- **New Workbook** means Excel pastes the output into a different workbook from the one containing the data. This is probably the least desirable option, as your data and statistical analyses will not be together in the same Excel file.

> **Tip:** When Excel pastes output into a spreadsheet, labels and values in the output may be cut off because the columns are not wide enough. To widen a column, position the mouse pointer over the divider to the right of the column. When the pointer changes to a cross ✛, hold down the primary mouse button and drag the column's edge to the right. Release the mouse button when everything is visible.

Summary statistics. Check this box in order for descriptive statistics to be calculated. Excel will produce the summary statistics shown in Figure 5.4.

Confidence level for mean. If this box is checked, Excel will calculate a 95% confidence interval around the mean. You can enter a different confidence level by deleting the 95 and entering a new value.

Kth largest and **Kth smallest.** These boxes are set to a default value of 1, meaning that Excel will return the minimum and maximum score in the data distribution. If you want the second largest and smallest values, check the box and enter 2 rather than 1. Most likely you have no need to change the default option.

Step 4: Interpret the Results of the Analysis

As shown in Figure 5.4, most descriptive statistics are provided. We will mention only a few here. The **mean** number of hours of TV watched per week is 12.64, with most individuals falling within a **standard deviation** of 3.96 hours around this sample mean. **Standard error** measures how much we expect the sample mean to deviate from the true population mean; we see that our sample mean has a **standard error** of 1.19.

Less familiar items are **kurtosis and skewness. Kurtosis** is an index of the shape of a distribution, describing how flat or peaked a curve is relative to a normal distribution. Negative values mean the distribution is flat, whereas positive values mean the distribution is peaked. **Skewness** is an index of the shape of a distribution, describing how asymmetrical the distribution is relative to a normal distribution. Negative values indicate a negatively skewed distribution; positive values indicate a positively skewed distribution. For both indices, values close to 0 indicate relatively normal-shaped distributions.

Figure 5.4
Output of the Descriptive Statistics procedure.

	A	B
1	*TV Hours*	
2		
3	Mean	12.63636
4	Standard Error	1.192955
5	Median	14
6	Mode	14
7	Standard Deviation	3.956583
8	Sample Variance	15.65455
9	Kurtosis	0.028861
10	Skewness	0.057829
11	Range	14
12	Minimum	6
13	Maximum	20
14	Sum	139
15	Count	11

Descriptive Statistics Using the Paste Function

Paste Function commands can also be used to find individual descriptive statistics, including those that are not produced by the **Analysis ToolPak's Descriptive Statistics** procedure. If you have missing values in your data, be sure to use the **Paste Function** commands, because the **Descriptive Statistics** procedure cannot handle missing data. Since all **Paste Function** commands work in a similar fashion, we will use only the calculation of the mean score as an example.

Step 1: Enter the Data

Enter a set of data for a variable down a column in an Excel spreadsheet. For illustration purposes, we will use the same data set as before on the number of hours of TV that 11 subjects estimated they watch per week (see Figure 5.1).

Step 2: Select a Cell and Activate the Paste Function

- Highlight the cell where you want the answer to appear in your spreadsheet.
- Click on the **Paste Function** icon ƒ∗ on the **Standard Toolbar** to open its menu.
- Highlight **Statistical**, as shown in Figure 5.5. You will see a set of statistical function names appear in the right scroll box. As you move the mouse cursor to highlight each statistical function name, the bottom of the dialog screen changes to tell you what that function does. In Figure 5.5, you see that the command **AVERAGE** calculates the mean of a set of numbers.

Figure 5.5
Paste Function
dialog box.

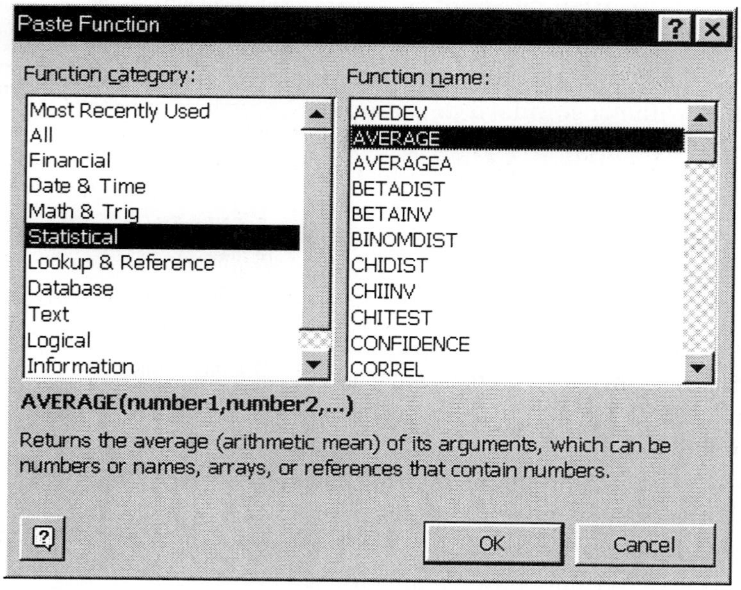

Step 3: Choose the Desired Statistical Function

- Highlight **AVERAGE** (for our example).
- Click on the **OK** button. As shown in Figure 5.6, a dialog box will appear for you to enter the cell range where your data are located. If in *Step 1* you highlighted a cell in the same column as your data, Excel will automatically fill in the dialog box with a cell range, but be sure to confirm that it is correct. In our example, the data can be

found in cells A2:A12. Once you have entered the cell range, Excel shows the answer to the formula in the bottom of the dialog box.

- Click the **OK** button and Excel will paste the answer into your original spreadsheet.

Figure 5.6
AVERAGE dialog box.

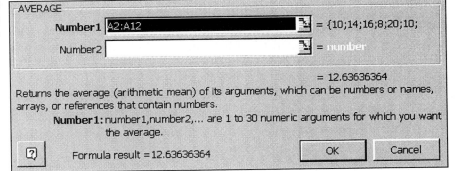

Step 4: Label the Output

In a cell immediately adjacent to the pasted statistical value, type a label indicating what summary statistic is contained in the cell (see Figure 5.7).

Figure 5.7
Labeling the value.

14	12.63636	Mean
15		

Special Notes on Paste Function

Finding Standard Deviation and Variance

A few words of caution on finding standard deviations and variances using Excel's built-in functions are necessary. Excel 97 contains four commands for standard deviation (**STDEV, STDEVA, STDEVP, STDEVPA**) and four commands for **variance (VAR, VARA, VARP, VARPA)**.

- If you want to calculate the *sample standard deviation* and *sample variance* (both use $n-1$ in the denominator), use **STDEV** and **VAR**.
- If you want the *population standard deviation* and the *population variance* (both use n in the denominator) use **STDEVP** and **VARP**.

You should never have need for the two other command forms.

Shortcut for Finding Descriptive Statistics

Once you are familiar with the built-in Excel function name for a statistic, you can type a formula directly into an active spreadsheet cell in your data using this method:

- Highlight a spreadsheet cell.
- Type **=FUNCTIONNAME(cell range)** and Excel pastes the answer into the cell.

For example,
=AVERAGE(A2:A10) returns the mean of the data in cells A2 to A10.
=STDEV(A2:A10) returns the sample standard deviation of the data in cells A2 to A10.

Step-by-Step Practice Exercise

1. Make up a set of quantitative data on a single variable. Use 15 cases and include at least one duplicate score (or else an error will result when Excel reports the mode). Label the data column with the name of the variable.

2. Find the summary statistics for your data variable using the **Analysis ToolPak** and save this output as a new worksheet named *Descriptives*.

3. Return to your original spreadsheet data located in Sheet 1. This time use the **Paste Function** to find the sample mean (**AVERAGE**) and sample standard deviation (**STDEV**). Paste the calculated values onto Sheet 1 somewhere near your column of data and label the output.

4. Compare the answers from Step 2 above with those from Step 3. Did you get the same value for the mean? The same sample standard deviation? If not, you made a mistake somewhere, most likely in entering cell ranges for the data, and you need to correct this.

5. Save the entire file using the name *Descriptives*.

One-Sample *t*-Test

The one-sample *t*-test is used when you want to compare a hypothesized value for the population mean with the mean of a single sample drawn from that population. Furthermore, in order to use this procedure the population standard deviation must be unknown (unlike a one-sample *z* test in which you have a known population standard deviation). For example, a manufacturer might claim that a particular model car gets 30 miles to the gallon, but no information about the standard deviation is provided. A sample of cars could then be drawn and their miles per gallon could be tested to see whether the data are consistent or inconsistent with the manufacturer's mileage claim.

In Excel, there is no **Analysis ToolPak** procedure for performing a one-sample *t*-test. Instead, the one-sample *t*-test can be calculated using a combination of built-in **Paste Function** statistical commands along with spreadsheet formulas. To understand the steps in this procedure, you need to know that the formula for a one-sample *t*-test is:

$$t = \frac{\overline{X} - \mu}{s / \sqrt{n}}$$

The numerator represents the difference between means and the denominator is the standard error of the sample mean. The symbols in the formula stand for:

- $\overline{X}$ is the sample mean.
- μ is the hypothesized population mean.
- s is the sample standard deviation based on the formula $\sqrt{SS / n - 1}$, where $SS =$ the sum of squared deviations from the sample mean.
- n is the sample size.

Steps for Calculating the One-Sample *t*-Test

Step 1: Enter the Data

Suppose you obtain a sample of 9 cars to test a car manufacturer's claim that one of its models averages 30 miles per gallon. Enter the data seen in Figure 6.1 into an Excel spreadsheet with Column A labeled *MPG*.

	A
Book1	
1	MPG
2	31
3	27
4	30
5	28
6	31
7	32
8	27
9	29
10	29
11	

Step 2: Label the Output

Widen column C and type in a series of labels to keep track of the statistical output that will be generated (see Figure 6.2). In the steps that follow, you will enter the result of each calculation into Column D next to its corresponding label.

C
ONE-SAMPLE t-TEST OUTPUT
Sample mean
Hypothesized population mean
Sample standard deviation
Sample size (count)
Difference between means
Standard error of the mean
Observed (calculated) t value
Degrees of freedom
Alpha level (which is usually .05, two-tailed)
Critical t value at chosen alpha level
Probability of observed (calculated) t

Step 3: Find the Sample Mean and Sample Standard Deviation

- Highlight the cell in column D adjacent to the label for the sample mean (cell D2 in the example).
- Click on the **Paste Function** icon f_x to find the sample mean (**AVERAGE**) and paste the answer into the cell that you highlighted.
- Highlight the cell in column D that is adjacent to the label for the sample standard deviation (cell D4 in the example).
- Use the **Paste Function** command to find the sample standard deviation (**STDEV**) and paste the answer into the cell that you highlighted.

Tip: The exact steps for finding means and standard deviations with the **Paste Function** are in *Chapter 5, Descriptive Statistics*.

Step 4: Enter the Sample Size and Hypothesized Population Mean

After performing the actions listed below, you should have a spreadsheet that looks like the one shown in Figure 6.3.

- Enter the value for the *Hypothesized population mean* into cell D3, which the manufacturer in our example claims to be 30 miles per gallon. The hypothesized mean is never a calculated value; it is derived from the research question at hand.
- Enter the sample size of 9 cars into cell D5, adjacent to the label *Sample size (count)*. If the sample size were large, you could use the **Paste Function COUNT** command to find the sample size for you, but here the small sample size of 9 is easily counted.

Figure 6.3
Appearance of
the spreadsheet
after completion
of Steps 3 and 4.

	A	B	C	D	E
1	MPG		ONE-SAMPLE t-TEST OUTPUT		
2	31		Sample mean	29.33333	
3	27		Hypothesized population mean	30	
4	30		Sample standard deviation	1.802776	
5	28		Sample size (count)	9	
6	31		Difference between means		
7	32		Standard error of the mean		
8	27		Observed (calculated) t value		
9	29		Degrees of freedom		
10	29		Alpha level (which is usually .05, two-tailed)		
11			Critical t value at chosen alpha level		
12			Probability of observed (calculated) t		
13					
14					

onesam_t — Sheet1 / Sheet2 / Sheet3

Step 5: Find the Mean Difference and Standard Error of the Mean

To simplify the equation, we need to find the values for the numerator (the mean difference) and the denominator (the standard error of the mean) of the one-sample *t* formula shown on the first page of this chapter.

To find the mean difference:
- Highlight the cell in column D adjacent to the label *Difference between Means* (cell D6 in the example).
- Type this formula in the highlighted cell: **=D2-D3**.
- Press the **ENTER** key. You have just subtracted the hypothesized population mean (in cell D3) from the sample mean (in cell D2).

To find the standard error of the mean:
- Highlight the cell adjacent to the label *Standard error of the mean* (cell D7).
- Type the following formula in the highlighted cell: **=D4/SQRT(D5)**. Standard error is found by dividing the standard deviation by the square root of the sample size, *n*. D4 is where the sample standard deviation is located, D5 is where the sample size is located and **SQRT** is Excel's **Paste Function** command for calculating square roots.
- Press the **ENTER** key.

Step 6: Find the Observed *t* Value

Cell D6 now contains the numerator and cell D7 contains the denominator of the one-sample *t* formula. To complete the calculation of *t* you need to divide these values, after which your spreadsheet should look like the one in Figure 6.4.

- Highlight the cell adjacent to the label *Observed (calculated) t value* (here, cell D8).
- Type in the formula: **=D6/D7**.
- Press the **ENTER** key.

	A	B	C	D	E
1	MPG		ONE-SAMPLE t-TEST OUTPUT		
2	31		Sample mean	29.33333	
3	27		Hypothesized population mean	30	
4	30		Sample standard deviation	1.802776	
5	28		Sample size (count)	9	
6	31		Difference between means	-0.66667	
7	32		Standard error of the mean	0.600925	
8	27		Observed (calculated) t value	-1.1094	
9	29		Degrees of freedom		
10	29		Alpha level (which is usually .05, two-tailed)		
11			Critical t value at chosen alpha level		
12			Probability of observed (calculated) t		
13					
14					

Sheet1 / Sheet2 / Sheet3 /

Step 7: Enter the Degrees of Freedom and the Alpha Level

Degrees of freedom (*df*) for a one-sample *t*-test are equal to the sample size (*n*) - 1 so here the degrees of freedom are 9-1= 8. Enter 8 in cell D9. The typical alpha level used in a hypothesis test is .05 two-tailed, though the research question sometime calls for a more stringent alpha, such as .01. Enter your chosen alpha level (.05 in this case) in cell D10. Entering degrees of freedom and alpha clarifies your output and reminds you about information needed to make a decision whether to reject or not reject the null hypothesis.

Step 8: Find the Critical *t* Value

To make a decision about the null hypothesis, you need the critical *t* value. You can use a table found in the back of statistics textbooks to look up the critical *t*, or you can let Excel find it. Excel has a built-in statistical function called **TINV** that returns the critical *t* value after you supply the desired alpha level and the associated degrees of freedom.

- Highlight the cell in column D adjacent to the label *Critical t value* (D11 in the example).
- Select the **Paste Function** icon *f*.
- Highlight **Statistical** in the left window, then scroll down the right side window and highlight **TINV**.
- Click the **OK** button; the dialog box shown in Figure 6.5 appears.
- Type in the desired alpha level, usually .05 two-tailed.

- Type in the degrees of freedom.
- Click the **OK** button to paste the critical *t* value into the cell you highlighted (D11).

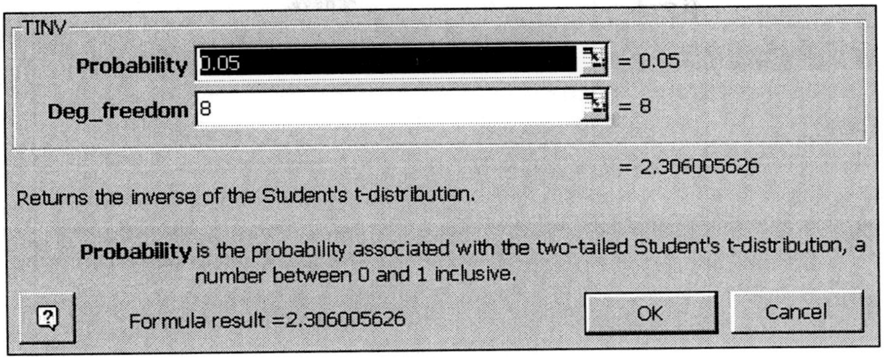

Figure 6.5
TINV Dialog box
for finding the
critical value of *t*.

Step 9: Find the Probability Value for Your Observed *t* Value

Statistical tables in most textbooks tell you only whether an observed *t* value is less than specific probability values such as .10, .05, or .01. The tables do not give the exact probability associated with the *t* value of the sample data. Excel has a built-in function for returning the exact probability value associated with any given *t* value.

- Highlight the cell adjacent to the label *Probability of observed (calculated) t value* (cell D12 in the example).
- Click on the **Paste Function** icon **f***.
- Highlight **Statistical** in the left window, then scroll down the right side window and highlight **TDIST**.
- Press the **OK** button; the dialog box in Figure 6.6 appears.

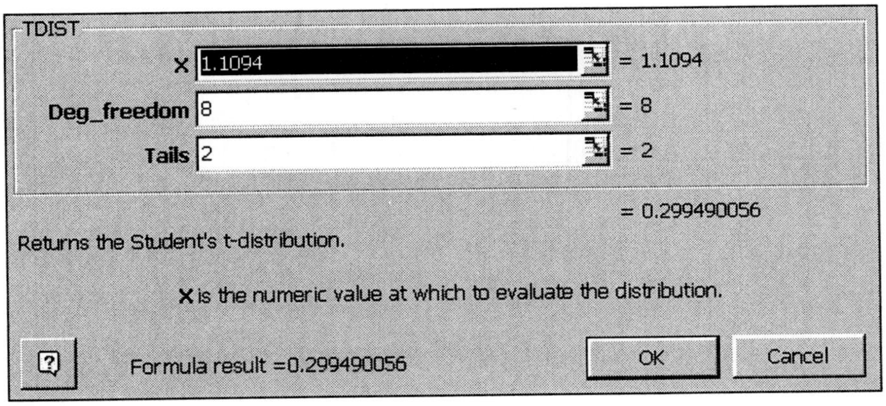

Figure 6.6
TDIST Dialog box
for finding the
probability
associated with
the observed *t*.

- Type in the observed *t* value calculated back in Step 6. You must enter a positive value (since a *t* distribution is symmetrical, positive and negative *t* values are equally distant from the mean of the distribution).
- Type in the degrees of freedom, which is 8 in our example.
- Type in a value of 1 if you wish the one-tailed probability value and a value of 2 if you wish the two-tailed probability value (which is more commonly used). Here, we typed in a 2.
- Click the **OK** button and Excel will paste the answer into the spreadsheet, which should now look like the one shown in Figure 6.7.

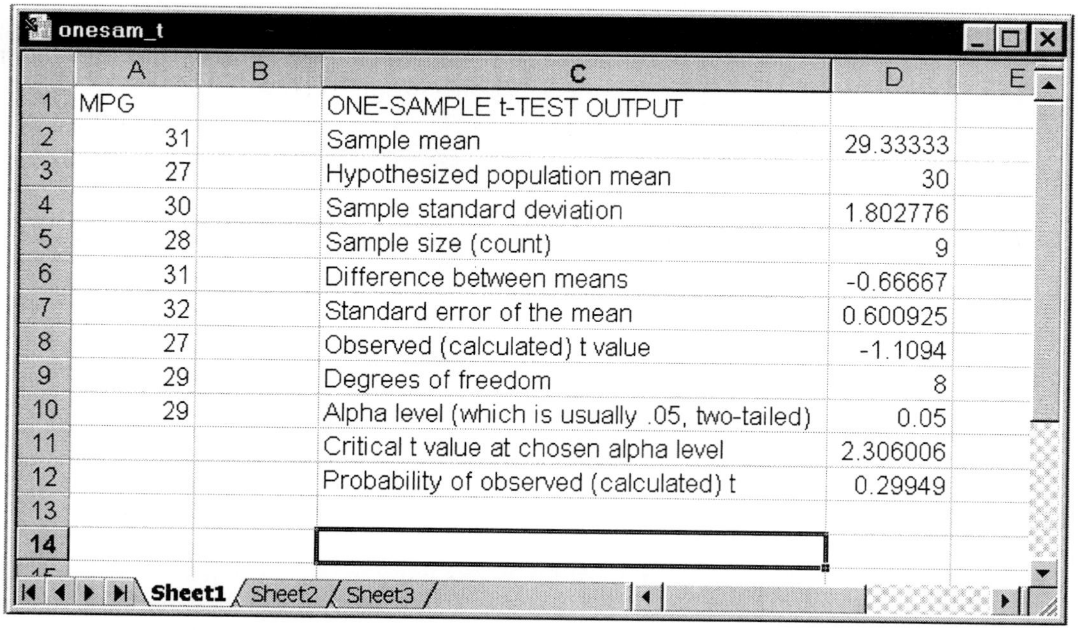

Figure 6.7
Appearance of
the spreadsheet
after completion
of Steps 7-9.

	A	B	C	D	E
1	MPG		ONE-SAMPLE t-TEST OUTPUT		
2	31		Sample mean	29.33333	
3	27		Hypothesized population mean	30	
4	30		Sample standard deviation	1.802776	
5	28		Sample size (count)	9	
6	31		Difference between means	-0.66667	
7	32		Standard error of the mean	0.600925	
8	27		Observed (calculated) t value	-1.1094	
9	29		Degrees of freedom	8	
10	29		Alpha level (which is usually .05, two-tailed)	0.05	
11			Critical t value at chosen alpha level	2.306006	
12			Probability of observed (calculated) t	0.29949	
13					
14					

onesam_t

Sheet1 / Sheet2 / Sheet3 /

Step 10: Interpret the Results of the Analysis

The observed t value of -1.1094 is less than the critical t value of ± 2.306 needed to reject the null hypothesis. Therefore, you would conclude that the observed sample mean of 29.33 miles per gallon was not significantly different from the manufacturer's claim of 30 mpg. You can also determine this from the fact that the observed t of -1.1094 has a probability of occurrence of $p = .2995$. This indicates that almost 30% of the time we could expect a sample mean ≤ 29.33 to occur, even if the true mileage is 30. In other words, our observed p value does not meet the alpha (significance) level of $p = .05$.

Note of caution: By default, Excel displays very small probability (p) values in scientific notation. If you happen to see a cell value such as 2.34E-06, this means you must move the decimal place six digits to the left to obtain the real value: $p = .00000234$.

Step-by-Step Practice Exercise

1. Make up a set of data that is appropriate for a one-sample t-test. Use 20 cases and label your variable.

2. To the side of your spreadsheet data, type in a brief description of your example and the research hypothesis being tested.

3. Follow the procedure described in this chapter to perform the one-sample t-test. Use alpha = .05, two-tailed as the significance level.

4. Beneath the output generated during the procedure, type an interpretation of the results. What conclusion can you draw from the data? Was the sample mean significantly greater than, less than, or no different than the hypothesized mean? What is your decision about the null vs. alternative hypothesis? How did you arrive at this decision?

5. Save your file using the name *One sample t*.

7

Independent-Samples *t*-Test

An independent-samples *t*-test is used to test hypotheses about two separate populations from which samples have been drawn and measured on a quantitative data variable. For example, researchers might wish to compare the behavior of an experimental treatment group with that of a control group, compare drug arrests in urban vs. suburban areas, or compare standardized test scores of students in private schools vs. public schools. The assumption is that the variability in both populations is the same (homogeneity of variance assumption) and that what you are trying to determine is whether the group means significantly differ.

Excel's **Analysis Toolpak** includes two procedures for performing an independent-samples *t*-test. One method (***t*-test: Two-Sample Assuming Equal Variances**) calculates the *t* value using standard formulas that assume the variances in the two groups are indeed approximately equal. The second method (***t*-test: Two-Sample Assuming Unequal Variances**) assumes the variances of the two groups are very unequal; its formulas compensate for violation of the *t*-test's homogeneity of variance assumption.

Unless you have very small (less than 25) or very unequal sample sizes, you are unlikely to violate the homogeneity of variance assumption. Therefore, this chapter will demonstrate how to use Excel's independent-samples *t*-test procedure for equal variances.

> **Tip:** If you should find yourself with unequal variances, the procedure you will follow differs from the directions here only in the initial choice of which independent t-test to use. Instead of ***t*-test: Two-Sample Assuming Equal Variances**, choose ***t*-test: Two-Sample Assuming Unequal Variances** from the **Data Analysis** dialog box in Step 2.

Steps for Calculating the Independent-Samples *t*-Test

Step 1: Enter the Data

Let us assume that a researcher wants to test the hypothesis that meditation training will help chronic pain patients. Compared to a control group of pain patients, the meditation group is predicted to consume fewer pain pills per day. The data in Figure 7.1 represent hypothetical scores from 12 subjects per group (although an independent-samples *t*-test does not require equal sample sizes).

Enter the data into an Excel spreadsheet and type column labels identifying the groups, as shown in Figure 7.1.

Figure 7.1
Pain pill consumption data.

	A	B
1	meditation group	control group
2	4	7
3	3	5
4	4	4
5	5	4
6	4	6
7	4	5
8	5	5
9	3	8
10	6	6
11	5	5
12	4	7
13	4	5
14		

Step 2: Choose the Analysis Procedure

- Click on **Tools** to drop down this menu.
- Click on **Data Analysis**.
- Scroll down and highlight *t*-**test: Two-Sample Assuming Equal Variances** in the **Data Analysis** dialog box (see Figure 7.2).
- Click on the **OK** button.

Figure 7.2
Data Analysis dialog box.

Data Analysis   **?** **X**

Analysis Tools

F-Test Two-Sample for Variances	OK
Fourier Analysis	
Histogram	Cancel
Moving Average	
Random Number Generation	Help
Rank and Percentile	
Regression	
Sampling	
t-Test: Paired Two Sample for Means	
t-Test: Two-Sample Assuming Equal Variances	

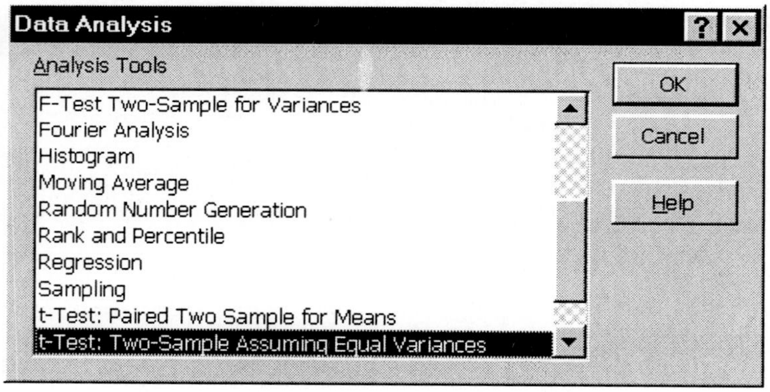

Step 3: Fill in the Dialog Box

Complete the dialog box as shown in Figure 7.3, then click the **OK** button to run the analysis.

Figure 7.3
Dialog box for
two independent-
samples *t*-Test.

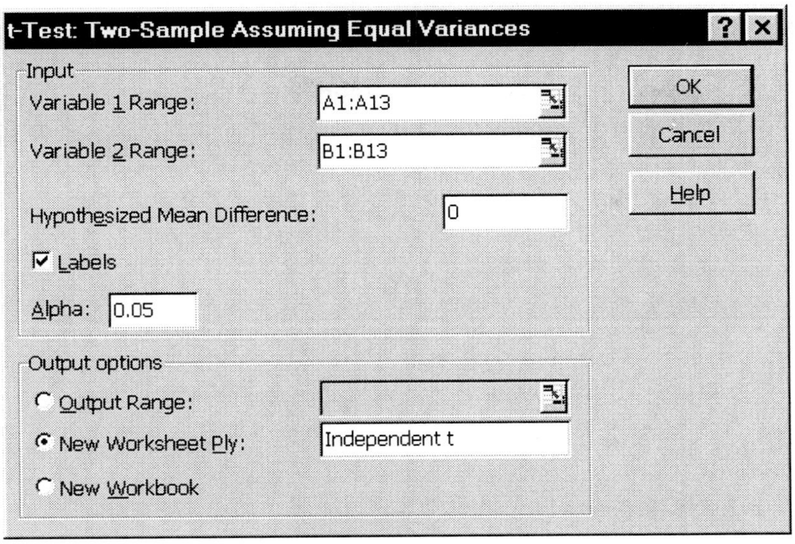

Input. Enter the cell locations of the data and label for the first group (cells A1:A13) in **Variable 1 Range**, and the cell locations of the data and label for the second group (cells B1:B13) in **Variable 2 Range**.

Hypothesized Mean Difference. The typical null hypothesis in an independent-samples *t*-test is that the two group means do not differ and that the mean difference is 0. Enter a 0 in this box.

Labels. Be sure to check this box so that group labels will be included with the output, making it more readable. When your input range includes the cell with your variable name, you must check this box or else Excel will give an error message.

Alpha. Accept the default significance level of .05, two-tailed unless you have a specific reason to change it based on your research hypothesis.

Output Options. Excel provides three choices for the output's location:
- **Output** Range places the output on the same spreadsheet page as your original data; you specify the cell location for the upper left corner of the output, e.g. cell D1.
- **New Worksheet Ply** is the default output location. Excel pastes the output into a new worksheet in the current workbook. Your data and output are kept together in the same file. You have the option to name the new worksheet by typing a name into the text box. If you do not name the new sheet, Excel will name it *Sheet 4,* or the next available name in the series (*Sheets 1, 2,* and *3* are created whenever you start a new Excel workbook). For our exercise, name the new sheet *Independent t*.
- **New Workbook** means Excel pastes the output into a different workbook from the one containing the data. This is probably the least desirable option, as your data and statistical analyses will not be together in the same Excel file.

Tip: When Excel pastes output into a spreadsheet, labels and values in the output may be cut off because the columns are not wide enough. To widen a column, position the mouse pointer over the divider to the right of the column. When the pointer changes to a cross ✛, hold down the primary mouse button and drag the column's edge to the right. Release the mouse button when everything is visible.

Step 4: Interpret the Results of the Analysis

After completing Step 3 and widening the columns, you should have output that looks like Figure 7.4. We'll focus on the important aspects of the results, but first examine the number of observations per group to ensure that all the data were analyzed.

Figure 7.4
Output of the
t-test procedure.

	A	B	C
1	t-Test: Two-Sample Assuming Equal Variances		
2			
3		*meditation group*	*control group*
4	Mean	4.25	5.583333333
5	Variance	0.75	1.537878788
6	Observations	12	12
7	Pooled Variance	1.143939394	
8	Hypothesized Mean Difference	0	
9	df	22	
10	t Stat	-3.05360497	
11	P(T<=t) one-tail	0.002911237	
12	t Critical one-tail	1.717144187	
13	P(T<=t) two-tail	0.005822473	
14	t Critical two-tail	2.073875294	

Mean. The output provides the sample means for each group. The meditation group consumed an average of 4.25 pills, with the control group consuming 5.58.

Variance. The output gives the variances for each sample (meditation group = .75; control group = 1.54). You should always calculate and report sample standard deviations. They are not computed here by Excel; however, they can be obtained easily. Either take the square root of each variance using a calculator, or use the **Paste Function SQRT** command. (See *Chapter 2, Spreadsheet Basics* for instructions on using Excel's **Paste Function** commands).

df. Degrees of freedom are located in cell B9. We had a total of 24 cases and we lose one *df* per group, so here we have a value of *df* = 22.

t stat. This is the observed *t* value in the data, calculated by applying the independent-samples *t*-test formula. It is located in cell B10; here the value reported is -3.054.

t Critical two-tail. This is the critical *t* value needed to reject the null hypothesis at the alpha level chosen when completing the dialog box in Step 3. We used alpha = .05, two-tailed. The critical *t* is located in cell B14; here the value reported is 2.074 (though this really means it is ± 2.074).

P(T<=*t*) two-tail. This is the two-tailed probability value associated with the observed *t*. It is located in cell B13; here the two-tailed *p* = .0058.

From these results we see that our observed *t* value of -3.054 exceeds the critical *t* value of ± 2.074. We also see that, if the null hypothesis were true, our results would be very unlikely to happen (our *p* = .0058, which is less than the .05 alpha level set as our cutoff for statistical significance). Therefore, the decision would be to reject the null hypothesis of no difference and assert that the groups do differ by more than chance. Finally, looking at the group means, we would state that the meditation group (*M* = 4.25) used significantly fewer pain pills per day than the control group (*M* = 5.58).

t **Critical one-tail and P(T<=*t*) one-tail.** The output also includes the critical *t* value for a one-tailed test of the null hypothesis (cell B12; here the value is 1.717) and the one-tailed probability value associated with the obtained *t* value (cell B11; here the value is .0029). One-tailed values should be used in situations where the researcher is employing a directional, one-tailed test of the null hypothesis rather than the more common non-directional, two-tailed test that we applied here.

> **Note of caution:** By default, Excel displays very small probability (*p*) values in scientific notation. If you happen to see a cell value such as 2.34E-06, this means you must move the decimal place six digits to the left to obtain the real value: *p* = .00000234.

Step-by-Step Practice Exercise

1. Make up a set of data that is appropriate for an independent-samples *t*-test and label your two groups. Use 15 scores per group.

2. To the side of your spreadsheet data, type in a brief description of your example and the research hypothesis being tested.

3. Use the **Analysis ToolPak *t*-test: Two-Sample Assuming Equal Variances** procedure to perform the independent-samples *t*-test. Use alpha = .05, two-tailed. Save the output on a new worksheet named *Independent t*.

4. Beneath the output generated by the procedure, type an interpretation of the results. What did you find out about the relationship between the independent and dependent variable? Include a decision about the null vs. alternative hypothesis. Identify the observed *t* value and its associated *p* value and the means for each group.

5. Identify the critical *t* value used to make a decision about the null hypothesis.

6. Save your file using the name *Independent t*.

Paired-Samples *t*-Test

The paired-samples *t*-test, also known as a correlated-groups *t*-test or dependent-groups *t*-test, assumes that you have pairs of data, which come either from a single sample or from matched subjects. For example, you might have a single sample that has been measured twice on the dependent variable, such as in a pretest-posttest design. Or, a single group of subjects might have been measured under two different treatment conditions as in a repeated measures design. Finally, subjects might have been matched on an existing variable and then measured on the data variable of interest. An example of the latter situation would be a case where you want to compare the performance of younger adults with older adults on a memory test. You might first pair subjects from the two age groups on variables like years of education or IQ score before administering the memory test.

Steps for Calculating the Paired-Samples *t*-Test

Step 1: Enter the Data

Imagine that a psychology student is interested in determining whether we react faster to a light stimulus or to a sound stimulus. A repeated measures design is used. Eight subjects are tested under each of two conditions: onset of a light stimulus and onset of a sound stimulus. The subject's task is to press a key as soon as the stimulus is presented. Reaction time is measured in milliseconds.

Enter the data and condition labels shown in Figure 8.1 in an Excel spreadsheet.

Figure 8.1
Response time data.

	A	B
	light	sound
1	light	sound
2	1505	1722
3	1843	1657
4	2109	1981
5	1670	1538
6	1826	1733
7	1815	2014
8	1598	1684
9	1779	1942
10		

Step 2: Choose the Analysis Procedure

- Click on **Tools** to drop down this menu.
- Click on **Data Analysis**.
- Scroll down and highlight **t-test: Paired Two Sample for Means** in the **Data Analysis** dialog box (see Figure 8.2).
- Click on the **OK** button.

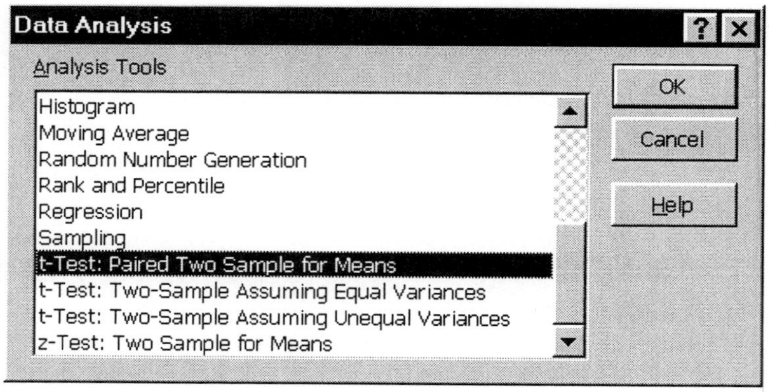

Figure 8.2
Data Analysis
dialog box.

Step 3: Fill in the Dialog Box

Complete the dialog box as shown in Figure 8.3 and click the **OK** button to run the analysis.

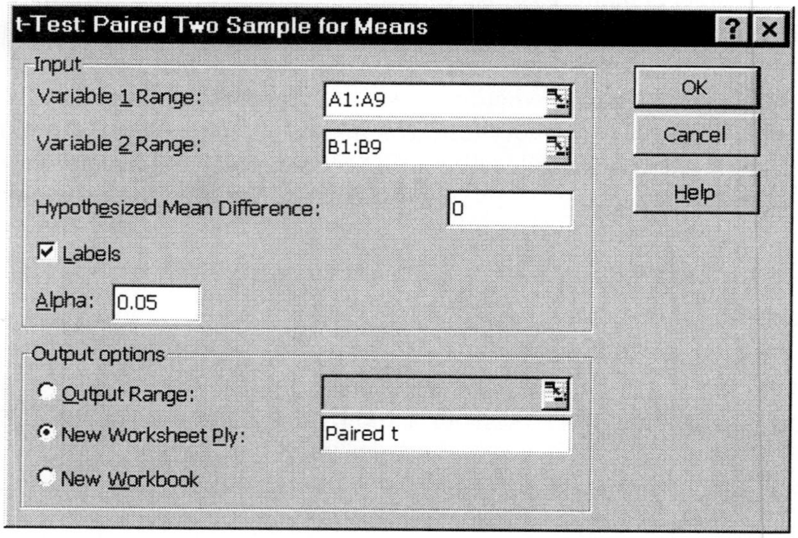

Figure 8.3
Paired-samples
t-test dialog box.

Input Range. Enter the cell locations of the data and variable label for the first score in each pair (here, cells A1:A9) in **Variable 1 Range**. Enter the cell locations of the data and variable label for the second score in each pair (here, cells B1:B9) in **Variable 2 Range**.

Hypothesized Mean Difference. The typical null hypothesis in a paired-samples *t*-test is that the two means do not differ and that the mean difference is 0. Enter a 0 in this box.

Labels. Be sure to check this box so that your column heading labels will be included with the output, making it more readable. Whenever your input range includes the cell with your variable name, you must check this box or else Excel will give an error message.

Alpha. Accept the default significance level of .05, two-tailed unless you have a specific reason to change it based on your research hypothesis.

Output Options. Excel provides three choices for the output's location:

- **Output** Range places the output on the same spreadsheet page as your original data; you specify the cell location for the upper left corner of the output, e.g. cell D1.
- **New Worksheet Ply** is the default output location. Excel pastes the output into a new worksheet in the current workbook. Your data and output are kept together in the same file. You have the option to name the new worksheet by typing a name into the text box. If you do not name the new sheet, Excel will name it *Sheet 4,* or the next available name in the series (*Sheets 1, 2,* and *3* are created whenever you start a new Excel workbook). For our exercise, name the new sheet *Paired t.*
- **New Workbook** means Excel pastes the output into a different workbook from the one containing the data. This is probably the least desirable option, as your data and statistical analyses will not be together in the same Excel file.

> **Tip:** When Excel pastes output into a spreadsheet, labels and values in the output may be cut off because the columns are not wide enough. To widen a column, position the mouse pointer over the divider to the right of the column. When the pointer changes to a cross ✛, hold down the primary mouse button and drag the column's edge to the right. Release the mouse button when everything is visible.

Step 4: Interpret the Results of the Analysis

After completing Step 3 and widening the columns, you should have output that looks like Figure 8.4. We will focus on the important aspects of the results, but we must first examine the number of observations for each condition to ensure that all the data were analyzed.

Figure 8.4
Output of the
t-test procedure.

	A	B	C	D
1	t-Test: Paired Two Sample for Means			
2				
3		*light*	*sound*	
4	Mean	1768.125	1783.875	
5	Variance	33610.41	29966.13	
6	Observations	8	8	
7	Pearson Correlation	0.56113		
8	Hypothesized Mean Difference	0		
9	df	7		
10	t Stat	-0.26641		
11	P(T<=t) one-tail	0.3988		
12	t Critical one-tail	1.894578		
13	P(T<=t) two-tail	0.797599		
14	t Critical two-tail	2.364623		

Mean. The output provides the sample means for each condition. The average reaction time to the light stimulus was 1768.13 milliseconds (msec); for the sound stimulus the average was 1783.88 msec.

Variance. The output gives the variances for each condition (light = 33610.41; sound = 29966.13). You should also always calculate and report sample standard deviations. They are not computed here by Excel; however, they can be obtained easily. Either take the square root of each variance using a calculator or use the **Paste Function SQRT** com-mand. (See *Chapter 2, Spreadsheet Basics* for instructions on using Excel's **Paste Func-tion** commands).

df. Degrees of freedom are located in cell B9. We had a single group of 8 subjects. We lose one *df* per group, so here we have a value of *df* = 7.

t **stat.** This is the observed *t* value in the data, calculated by applying the paired-samples *t*-test formula. It is located in cell B10; here the value reported is -.266.

t **Critical two-tail.** This is the critical *t* value needed to reject the null hypothesis at the alpha level chosen when completing the dialog box in Step 3. We used alpha = .05, two-tailed. The critical *t* is located in cell B14; here the value reported is 2.365 (though this really means it is ± 2.365).

P(T<=*t*) two-tail. This is the two-tailed probability value associated with the observed *t*. It is located in cell B13; here the two-tailed *p* = .798.

From these results, we see that our observed *t* value of -.266 does not meet the critical *t* value of ± 2.365 needed to reject the null hypothesis. The *p* = .798 tells us that our ob-served *t* value would happen about 80% of the time if the null hypothesis were true, which is far more often than the 5% alpha level set as our cutoff for statistical signifi-cance. Therefore, the decision would be to retain the null hypothesis of no difference and assert that reaction time to light stimuli (*M* = 1768.125 msec) and sound stimuli (*M* = 1783.875 msec) did not differ significantly.

t **Critical one-tail and P(T<=*t*) one-tail.** The output also includes the critical *t* value for a one-tailed test of the null hypothesis (cell B12; here the value is 1.895) and the one-tailed probability value associated with the obtained *t* value (cell B11; here the value is .3988). One-tailed values should be used in situations where the researcher is employing a directional, one-tailed test of the null hypothesis rather than the more common non-directional, two-tailed test that we applied here.

> **Note of caution:** By default, Excel displays very small probability (*p*) values in scientific notation. If you happen to see a cell value such as 2.34E-06, this means you must move the decimal place six digits to the left to obtain the real value: *p* = .00000234.

Step-by-Step Practice Exercise

1. Make up a set of data that is appropriate for a paired-samples *t*-test and label your two conditions. Use 15 scores per column.

2. To the side of your spreadsheet data, type in a brief description of your example and the research hypothesis being tested.

3. Use the **Analysis ToolPak t-test: Paired Two Sample for Means** procedure to per-form the paired-samples *t*-test. Use alpha = .05, two-tailed. Save the output on a new worksheet named *Paired t*.

4. Beneath the output generated by the procedure, type an interpretation of the results. What did you find out about the relationship between the independent and dependent variable? Include a decision about the null vs. alternative hypothesis. Identify the observed *t* value and its associated *p* value and the means for each condition.

5. Identify the critical *t* value used to make a decision about the null hypothesis.

6. Save your file using the name *Paired t*.

9

One-Way ANOVA for Independent Samples

A one-way or single-factor analysis of variance (ANOVA) is used in situations where there is one independent variable, also known as a factor. Unlike a *t*-test, which can only compare two levels of the independent variable, a one-way ANOVA can be used to compare any number of groups or conditions. The specific ANOVA procedure described below assumes that the data come from separate, independent samples, such as in a between-groups research design.

The Excel analysis generates descriptive statistics and an ANOVA summary table. It computes an *F* ratio, which is used to determine whether any of the conditions significantly differed. If the *F* value is statistically significant and there are more than two levels of the independent variable, pairwise comparisons using a procedure like the Scheffé test or the Tukey test need to be performed. These procedures compare each possible pair of means to determine exactly where the mean differences occur. You will need to refer to a statistics textbook for these; Excel does not include any such statistical techniques.

Steps for Calculating the One-Way ANOVA for Independent Samples

Step 1: Enter the Data

Assume that the campaign manager for a politician has hired a researcher to assess the effectiveness of three commercials planned for the candidate. They wish to determine which commercial results in the most favorable attitude toward the candidate. Subjects are randomly assigned to watch one of three ads, with 11 subjects watching the first ad, 12 subjects watching the second ad, and 12 subjects watching the third ad. Afterward, each subject answers a questionnaire about attitudes toward the candidate. The highest possible score on the questionnaire is 35, and a score of 20 indicates a neutral attitude.

Enter the data shown in Figure 9.1.

Figure 9.1
Commercial effectiveness data.

	A	B	C
	Ad 1	Ad 2	Ad 3
1	Ad 1	Ad 2	Ad 3
2	22	28	22
3	28	29	27
4	25	30	23
5	22	31	22
6	21	28	30
7	24	27	25
8	23	22	30
9	23	28	21
10	20	32	24
11	26	26	25
12	23	25	28
13		30	22
14			

Step 2: Choose the Analysis Procedure

- Click on **Tools** to drop down this menu.
- Click on **Data Analysis**.
- Scroll down and highlight **ANOVA: Single-Factor** in the **Data Analysis** dialog box (see Figure 9.2).
- Click on the **OK** button.

Figure 9.2
Data Analysis
dialog box.

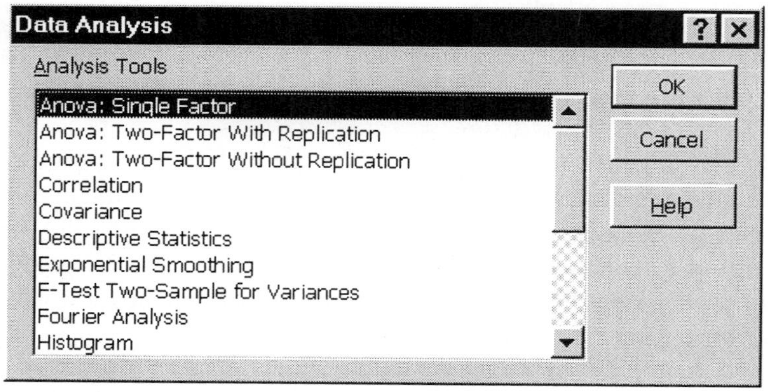

Step 3: Fill in the Dialog Box

Complete the dialog box as shown in Figure 9.3 and click the **OK** button to run the analysis.

Figure 9.3
ANOVA: Single
Factor dialog box.

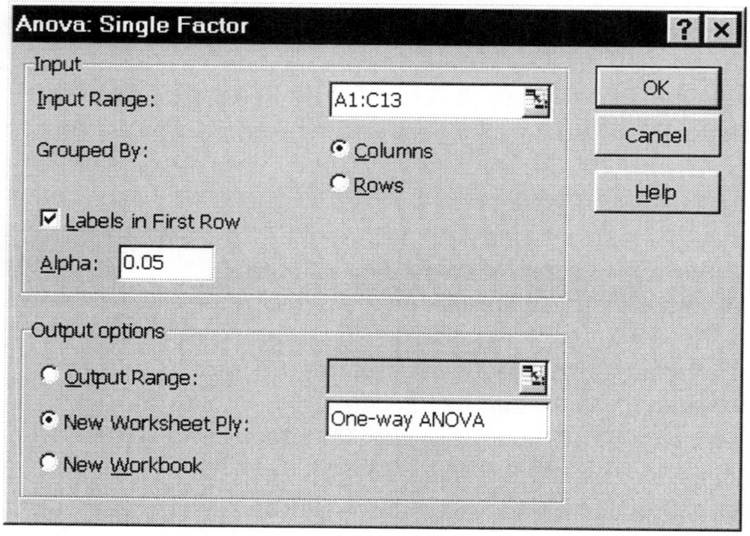

Input Range. Enter the cell locations of all data, including group labels. In the example, the range is cell A1:C13.

Grouped By. Indicate whether your data for each condition are found down a column or across a row. Data entry in Excel is typically in column format so this is already marked as the default option.

Labels. Be sure to check this box so that your group names will be included with the output. Whenever your input range includes the cells with your column headings, you must check this box or else Excel will give an error message.

Alpha. Accept the default significance level of .05 unless you have a specific reason to change it based on your research hypothesis.

Output Options. Excel provides three choices for the output's location:

- **Output Range** places the output on the same spreadsheet page as your original data; you specify the cell location for the upper left corner of the output, e.g. cell D1.
- **New** Worksheet is the default output location. Excel pastes the output into a new worksheet in the current workbook. Your data and output are kept together in the same file. You have the option to name the new worksheet by typing a name into the text box. If you do not name the new sheet, Excel will name it *Sheet 4,* or the next available name in the series (*Sheets 1, 2,* and *3* are created whenever you start a new Excel workbook). For our exercise, name the new sheet *One-way ANOVA.*
- **New Workbook** means Excel pastes the output into a different workbook from the one containing the data. This is probably the least desirable option, as your data and statistical analyses will not be together in the same Excel file.

> **Tip:** When Excel pastes output into a spreadsheet, labels and values in the output may be cut off because the columns are not wide enough. To widen a column, position the mouse pointer over the divider to the right of the column. When the pointer changes to a cross ✛, hold down the primary mouse button and drag the column's edge to the right. Release the mouse button when everything is visible.

Step 4: Interpret the Results of the Analysis

After completing Step 3 and widening columns, you should have output that looks like Figure 9.4. The output includes the summary statistics for each group as well as the analysis of variance summary table. We will focus on the important aspects of the results, but first examine the count of observations per group to ensure that all the data were analyzed.

Summary statistics. As shown in Figure 9.4, the mean and variance for each condition are generated. You can see that the highest mean ($M = 28$) is for advertisement 2 and the lowest mean ($M = 23.36$) is for advertisement 1. You should always calculate and report the sample standard deviations for each group. Excel does not report them here, but you can obtain them easily. Either find the square root of each variance using a calculator, or use the **Paste Function SQRT** command. (See *Chapter 2, Spreadsheet Basics* for instructions on using Excel's **Paste Function** commands).

ANOVA summary table.

- **Source of variation.** The *Total* variation is partitioned into *Between Groups* and *Within Groups. Between Groups* represents variability due to treatment differences: type of advertisement in our example. *Within Groups* represents random or natural variation in the dependent variable, such as variation caused by individual differences or experimental error.
- **df.** The degrees of freedom for *Between Groups* and *Within Groups* are provided. There were three groups in our example, so *df Between Groups* = 2: one less than the

number of groups. There were 35 subjects divided across 3 treatment groups, so *df Within Groups* = 32: We lose one degree of freedom from each group's sample size.

- **F.** This is the observed *F* ratio in the data, calculated by dividing *MS Between Groups* by *MS Within Groups*. It is located in cell E12; here the value obtained is 8.359.
- **F crit.** This is the critical *F* value needed to reject the null hypothesis at the alpha level chosen when completing the dialog box in Step 3. We used alpha = .05. The critical *F* is located in cell G12; here it is 3.294.
- **P-value.** This is the probability value associated with the observed *F* ratio. It is located in cell F12; here *p* = .0012. (Unlike the *t* distribution, which is symmetrical, the *F* distribution is positively skewed, so all probability values are one-tailed).

Figure 9.4
Output of the one-way ANOVA.

	A	B	C	D	E	F	G
1	Anova: Single Factor						
2							
3	SUMMARY						
4	*Groups*	*Count*	*Sum*	*Average*	*Variance*		
5	Ad 1	11	257	23.36364	5.254545		
6	Ad 2	12	336	28	7.636364		
7	Ad 3	12	299	24.91667	10.08333		
8							
9							
10	ANOVA						
11	*Source of Variation*	*SS*	*df*	*MS*	*F*	*P-value*	*F crit*
12	Between Groups	129.2807	2	64.64037	8.358822	0.001201	3.294531
13	Within Groups	247.4621	32	7.733191			
14							
15	Total	376.7429	34				

From these results we see that our observed *F* of 8.359 exceeds the critical *F* of 3.294 needed to reject the null hypothesis. The small *p* value of .0012 means that our observed *F* ratio would hardly ever occur if the null hypothesis were true. Therefore, the decision would be to reject the null hypothesis of no difference and assert that attitudes toward the advertisements do significantly differ. Looking at the means for each campaign commercial leads to the conclusion that the second ad (*M* = 28) produced significantly more positive attitudes toward the candidate than the first ad (*M* = 23.36) or the third ad (*M* = 24.92). (To determine whether the difference between each mean pair is significant, you will either have to manually perform a procedure such as the Scheffé test or the Tukey test, or else use other statistical software).

Note of caution: By default, Excel displays very small probability (*p*) values in scientific notation. If you happen to see a cell value such as 2.34E-06, this means you must move the decimal place six digits to the left to obtain the real value: *p* = .00000234.

Step-by-Step Practice Exercise

1. Make up a set of data containing three groups or conditions of a single independent variable. The data must come from three separate samples, not from related groups. Use 10 scores per group and label each column of data.

2. To the side of your spreadsheet data, type in a brief description of your example and the research hypothesis being tested.

3. Use the **Analysis ToolPak ANOVA: Single-Factor** procedure to perform a one-way ANOVA for independent samples. Use alpha = .05. Save the output on a new worksheet named *Oneway*.

4. Beneath the output generated by the procedure, type an interpretation of the results. What did you find out about the relationship between the independent and dependent variable? Include a decision about the null vs. alternative hypothesis. Identify the observed *F* value and its associated *p* value and the means for each group.

5. Identify the critical *F* value used to make a decision about the null hypothesis.

6. Save your file using the name *Oneway*.

One-Way Repeated Measures ANOVA

A one-way repeated measures analysis of variance (ANOVA) is used in situations where there is one treatment factor or independent variable, and the data come from correlated groups or from the same sample measured under all conditions. In other words, this procedure is used in situations similar to the paired *t*-test (*see Chapter 8*), except it is generally applied when there are three or more levels of the independent variable. A good example of this is a longitudinal research design. A researcher specializing in language development might examine age changes in language acquisition in the same group of infants at 6 months of age, 9 months of age, 12 months of age, and again at 15 months of age. A one-way repeated measures ANOVA could then be used to examine differences in specific language skills measured across the four age levels.

The Excel analysis generates descriptive statistics and an ANOVA summary table. It computes an *F* ratio, which is used to determine whether performance on a dependent variable varied across treatment conditions. If the *F* value is statistically significant and there are more than two levels of the independent variable, pairwise comparisons using a procedure like the Scheffé test or the Tukey test need to be performed. These procedures compare each possible pair of means to determine exactly where the mean differences occur. You will need to refer to a statistics textbook for these; Excel does not contain any such statistical techniques.

Steps for Calculating the One-Way Repeated Measures ANOVA

Step 1: Enter the Data

Suppose that a psychologist is interested in studying the effects of sleep deprivation on attention, perception, and motor skills. Performance on a video game serves as the dependent variable, and each subject's score is taken three times. The highest possible score on the video game is 1,000 points. The first score is taken after the person has been deprived of sleep for 24 hours, then again at 36 and 48 hours. Subjects are not allowed to practice the video game between intervals.

Start a new Excel spreadsheet and enter the three video game scores for each subject (see Figure 10.1). We also need a column for subjects' name, though cases could just as easily be identified by number or code.

Figure 10.1
Data resulting from the sleep deprivation study.

	A	B	C	D
1	Subject	24 hours	36 hours	48 hours
2	Jane	811	798	689
3	John	605	625	501
4	Jerry	753	734	707
5	Judy	822	845	781
6	Jed	516	554	522
7	Jason	682	663	619
8	Joan	772	761	728
9	Jenny	559	563	565

Step 2: Choose the Analysis Procedure

Excel's name for a one-way repeated measures ANOVA (**Anova: Two-Factor Without Replication**) is unusual, particularly for those in the field of social and behavioral sciences. The name relates to the fact that Excel will display an ANOVA summary table showing a *Rows* (subjects) factor and a *Columns* (treatments) factor. We describe this further when interpreting the output in Step 4. Perform the actions listed:

- Click on **Tools** to drop down this menu.
- Click on **Data Analysis**.
- Scroll down and highlight **Anova: Two-Factor Without Replication** in the **Data Analysis** dialog box (see Figure 10.2).
- Click on the **OK** button.

Figure 10.2
Data Analysis dialog box.

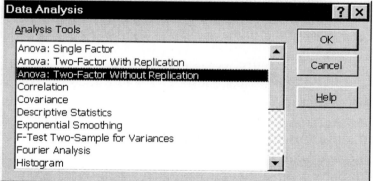

Step 3: Fill in the Dialog Box

Complete the dialog box, as shown in Figure 10.3, and click the **OK** button to run the analysis.

Input Range. Enter or highlight the cell locations of all data, including your column labels. In the example, the range is A1:D9.

Labels. Be sure to check this

Figure 10.3
One-way repeated measures ANOVA dialog box.

box so that your column labels will be included with the output. Whenever your input range includes the cells with your column headings, you must check this box or else Excel will give an error message.

Alpha. Accept the default significance level of .05 unless you have a specific reason to change it based on your research hypothesis.

Output Options. Excel provides three choices for the output's location:
- **Output Range** places the output on the same spreadsheet page as your original data; you specify the cell location for the upper left corner of the output, e.g. cell D1.
- **New Worksheet** is the default output location. Excel pastes the output into a new worksheet in the current workbook. Your data and output are kept together in the same file. You have the option to name the new worksheet by typing a name into the text box. If you do not name the new sheet, Excel will name it *Sheet 4,* or the next available name in the series (*Sheets 1, 2* and *3* are created whenever you start a new Excel workbook). For our exercise, name the new sheet *Repeated*.
- **New Workbook** means Excel pastes the output into a different workbook from the one containing the data. This is probably the least desirable option, as your data and statistical analyses will not be together in the same Excel file.

> **Tip:** When Excel pastes output into a spreadsheet, labels and values in the output may be cut off because the columns are not wide enough. To widen a column, position the mouse pointer over the divider to the right of the column. When the pointer changes to a cross ✛, hold down the primary mouse button and drag the column's edge to the right. Release the mouse button when everything is visible.

Step 4: Interpret the Results of the Analysis

After completing Step 3 and widening the columns, you should have output that looks like Figures 10.4 and 10.5. The output includes the summary statistics as well as the analysis of variance summary table. We will focus on the important aspects of the results, but first examine the number of observations in the *Count* column to ensure that all the data were analyzed.

Summary statistics. As shown in Figure 10.4, the mean and variance for each subject and for each condition are generated. The descriptive statistics for each condition, not each subject, are of primary interest. You can see that the lowest average score on the video game occurred after 48 hours of sleep deprivation ($M = 639$). The mean scores for the 24-hour sleep deprivation condition ($M = 690$) and the 36-hour sleep deprivation condition ($M = 692.875$) are roughly equal.

You should always calculate and report the sample standard deviations for each group. Excel does not report them here, but you can obtain them easily. Either find the square root of each variance using a calculator, or use the **Paste Function SQRT** command. (See *Chapter 2, Spreadsheet Basics* for instructions on using Excel's **Paste Function** commands).

Figure 10.4
Summary
statistics.

	A	B	C	D	E
1	Anova: Two-Factor Without Replication				
2					
3	SUMMARY	Count	Sum	Average	Variance
4	Jane	3	2298	766	4489
5	John	3	1731	577	4432
6	Jerry	3	2194	731.3333	534.3333
7	Judy	3	2448	816	1051
8	Jed	3	1592	530.6667	417.3333
9	Jason	3	1964	654.6667	1044.333
10	Joan	3	2261	753.6667	524.3333
11	Jenny	3	1687	562.3333	9.333333
12					
13	24 hours	8	5520	690	13926.29
14	36 hours	8	5543	692.875	11739.84
15	48 hours	8	5112	639	10545.43

ANOVA summary table. The repeated measures analysis of variance summary table (see Figure 10.5) is more complicated to read than the ANOVA table from an independent samples procedure (see *Chapter 9*).

- **Source of variation.** The *Total* variation is partitioned into *Rows, Columns,* and *Error*. Each row in the spreadsheet represented data from a single case or subject; therefore, the *Rows* factor represents variability due to individual differences. Each spreadsheet column represents the entire group's data; therefore, the *Columns* factor represents variability due to treatment differences (i.e., amount of sleep deprivation in our example). The *Error* term is the Subjects x Treatments interaction, and will be used in the denominator of each *F* ratio.

- **Interpretation of the *Rows* factor.** Notice that there are two *F* ratios shown in the ANOVA summary table, one for the *Rows* (subjects) factor and one for the *Columns* (treatments) factor. The *F* value associated with the *Rows* (subjects) factor does not address the research question and is not even mentioned when reporting research results. Here, the significant *F* value of 47.19 found in cell E20 simply tells us that some subjects were better at the video game than others. Hardly surprising!

- **Interpretation of the *Columns* factor.** The *F* value of interest is the one associated with the *Columns* (treatment) factor because this answers the question of whether video game performance varied across sleep deprivation conditions. This observed *F* ratio of 9.98 is found in cell E21, and clearly exceeds the critical *F* value of 3.74 (located in cell G21) needed for statistical significance. The *p* value for the *Columns* (treatments) *F* ratio is found in cell F21 and is .002. Our decision would be to reject the null hypothesis of no difference and assert that video game performance was affected by the amount of sleep deprivation. Looking at the means for each condition (see Figure 10.4), it appears that 48 hours of sleep deprivation led to significantly poorer video game scores ($\underline{M}$ = 639), but there was no real decrease in performance between 24 hours ($\underline{M}$ = 690) and 36 hours ($\underline{M}$ = 692.9). (To determine whether the difference between each mean pair is significant, you will either have to manually perform a procedure like the Scheffé test or the Tukey test, or else use other statistical software. Excel does not include any such procedures).

Figure 10.5
ANOVA summary
table.

	A	B	C	D	E	F	G
18	ANOVA						
19	*Source of Variation*	*SS*	*df*	*MS*	*F*	*P-value*	*F crit*
20	Rows	243175.6	7	34739.38	47.19451	1.13E-08	2.764196
21	Columns	14698.08	2	7349.042	9.9839	0.00202	3.73889
22	Error	10305.25	14	736.0893			
23							
24	Total	268179	23				

Note of caution: By default, Excel displays very small probability (p) values in scientific notation. For example, the p value associated with the Rows (subjects) factor in cell F20 is listed as 1.13E-08. E-08 means that you must move the decimal place eight digits to the left to obtain the real value: p = .0000000113.

Step-by-Step Practice Exercise

1. Make up a set of data containing three groups or conditions of a single independent variable. The data must come from three related samples, not from independent groups. Use 10 scores per group and label each column of data.

2. To the side of your spreadsheet data, type in a brief description of your example and the research hypothesis being tested.

3. Use the **Analysis ToolPak's Anova: Two-Factor Without Replication** procedure to perform a one-way ANOVA for repeated measures. Use alpha = .05. Save the output on a new worksheet named *Repeated*.

4. Beneath the output generated by the procedure, type an interpretation of the results. What did you find out about the relationship between the independent and dependent variable? Include a decision about the null vs. alternative hypothesis. Identify the observed F value and its associated p value and the means for each group.

5. Identify the critical F value used to make a decision about the null hypothesis.

6. Save your file using the name *Repeated*.

11

Two-Factor ANOVA for Independent Samples

In *Chapter 9* and *Chapter 10* we illustrated the use of one-way analysis of variance (ANOVA), which looks at the effect of a single independent variable on the dependent variable. It is also possible to have *factorial research designs* that include two, three, or more independent variables. A two-way or two-factor ANOVA looks at the separate effects of two independent variables on the dependent variable, as well as their combined effect, which is known as an interaction.

For example, a biomedical researcher comparing the effects of two medications might administer Drug A to one group and Drug B to another group. Simultaneously, the researcher might want to determine which dosage is most effective and therefore manipulate dosage levels of each drug, using 50 milligrams, 100 mg, and 150 mg. This would result in a 2 (Drug Type) x 3 (Dosage Level) factorial design, with six groups needed for the study (Drug A at 50 mg, Drug B at 50 mg, etc.). The researcher would then be able to assess the separate or main effect of each independent variable. Was one drug more effective than another? Was a certain dosage level more effective than another? The researcher would also be able to examine the interaction effect. For example, was one drug more effective at a low dosage but the other more effective at a high dosage?

The only type of factorial design for which Excel has a built-in analysis is two-factor ANOVA for independent samples. In other words, both factors must be between-groups, where each subject is included in only one condition or group. Moreover, Excel's procedure is limited to instances where all group sizes are equal. For more complex factorial designs, you need to use advanced statistical software like SPSS (Statistical Package for the Social Sciences).

Steps for Calculating the Two-Factor ANOVA for Independent Samples

Step 1: Enter the Data

Suppose that in an experiment on creativity, college students were asked to compose a poem. Half the subjects were told that their poetry would be evaluated for creativity and that they would be shown the judges' comments. The other half was told that the purpose of the poem was to provide a handwriting sample for analysis. The researcher was primarily interested in seeing whether creativity would be affected by the expectation that one's work is being evaluated. A second purpose for the study was to compare male vs. female creativity scores. This resulted in four separate groups in a 2 (Gender) x 2

(Expectation Condition) factorial design. To score the data, the researcher had poetry experts who were blind to the subject's gender and expectation condition rate each poem for creativity.

Enter the information shown in Figure 11.1 into an Excel spreadsheet. Labels for all levels of the Row factor and the Column factor *must* be included in the format illustrated; labels were desirable but optional in the previous analyses we have discussed. Be sure to sort the Row factor data. In our example, Gender is the Row factor; all the males' data were entered, then the females' data.

Figure 11.1
Data resulting from the study of creativity.

	A	B	C
1	Gender	Evaluation Expected	No Evaluation Expected
2	Male	16	21
3	Male	18	19
4	Male	21	22
5	Male	16	23
6	Male	15	21
7	Male	17	20
8	Female	18	23
9	Female	19	22
10	Female	18	23
11	Female	16	19
12	Female	15	22
13	Female	20	21

Step 2: Choose the Analysis Procedure

Excel's name for the two-factor ANOVA for independent samples (**Anova: Two-Factor With Replication**) is unusual, particularly for those in the field of social and behavioral sciences. The name relates to the fact that Excel will display an ANOVA summary table showing a *Sample* factor and a *Columns* factor. The name of the analysis implies that the treatment conditions being compared (e.g., evaluation expected vs. no evaluation expected) are replicated on different samples (a male sample and a female sample in our example). In practice, the *Sample* factor can represent either an existing subject characteristic like gender or a manipulated variable such as type of feedback given to subjects: positive vs. negative. Perform the actions listed:

- Click on **Tools** to drop down this menu.
- Click on **Data Analysis**.
- Scroll down and highlight **Anova: Two-Factor With Replication** in the **Data Analysis** dialog box (see Figure 11.2).
- Click on the **OK** button.

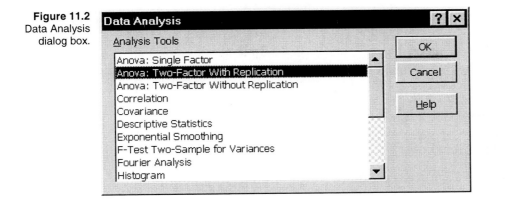

Figure 11.2
Data Analysis
dialog box.

Step 3: Fill in the Dialog Box

Complete the dialog box as shown in Figure 11.3, and click the **OK** button to run the analysis.

Figure 11.3
Two-factor
ANOVA dialog
box.

Input Range. Enter or highlight the cell locations of the data, including row and column labels. In the example, the range is A1:C13. Excel cannot do the analysis if the labels are missing.

Rows per sample. There must be the same number of rows for each level of the *Sample* (Rows) factor. Excel cannot compute a two-factor ANOVA if the group sizes are unequal. In our case, we have 6 male subjects and 6 female subjects per treatment condition so we would enter a 6 here.

Alpha. Accept the default significance level of .05 unless you have a specific reason to change it based on your research hypothesis.

Output Options. Excel provides three choices for the output's location:
- **Output Range** places the output on the same spreadsheet page as your original data; you specify the cell location for the upper left corner of the output, e.g. cell D1.
- **New Worksheet Ply** is the default output location. Excel pastes the output into a new worksheet in the current workbook. Your data and output are kept together in the same file. You have the option to name the new worksheet by typing a name into the text box. If you do not name the new sheet, Excel will name it *Sheet 4,* or the next

available name in the series (*Sheets 1, 2,* and *3* are created whenever you start a new Excel workbook). For our exercise, name the new sheet *Twofactor*.

- **New Workbook** means Excel pastes the output into a different workbook from the one containing the data. This is probably the least desirable option, as your data and statistical analyses will not be together in the same Excel file.

> **Tip:** When Excel pastes output into a spreadsheet, labels and values in the output may be cut off because the columns are not wide enough. To widen a column, position the mouse pointer over the divider to the right of the column. When the pointer changes to a cross ✛, hold down the primary mouse button and drag the column's edge to the right. Release the mouse button when everything is visible.

Step 4: Interpret the Results of the Analysis

After completing Step 3 and widening columns, you should have output that looks like Figures 11. 4 and 11.5. The output includes the summary statistics as well as the analysis of variance summary table. We will focus on the important aspects of the results, but first examine the number of observations in each row labeled *Count* to ensure that all the data were analyzed.

Figure 11.4 Summary statistics.

	A	B	C	D
1	Anova: Two-Factor With Replication			
2				
3	SUMMARY	Evaluation Expected	No Evaluation Expected	Total
4	*Male*			
5	Count	6	6	12
6	Sum	103	126	229
7	Average	17.16666667	21	19.08333
8	Variance	4.566666667	2	6.992424
9				
10	*Female*			
11	Count	6	6	12
12	Sum	106	130	236
13	Average	17.66666667	21.66666667	19.66667
14	Variance	3.466666667	2.266666667	6.969697
15				
16	*Total*			
17	Count	12	12	
18	Sum	209	256	
19	Average	17.41666667	21.33333333	
20	Variance	3.71969697	2.060606061	
21				

Summary statistics. Figure 11.4 shows the means and variances for all four groups, along with the *Total* means and variances for each level of the *Sample* (Rows) and *Columns* factors. For example, reading across row 7, we see that for males who expected to be evaluated, $M = 17.17$; for males not expecting to be evaluated, $M = 21$; and for males as a whole, $M = 19.08$. Reading across row 13 you find the mean creativity scores for females. The figures presented in row 19 indicate the mean creativity score for each condition (evaluation expected, evaluation not expected) including data from *both* the male and female samples.

You should always calculate and report the sample standard deviations for each group. Excel does not report them here, but you can obtain them easily. Either find the square root of each variance using a calculator, or use the **Paste Function SQRT** command. (See *Chapter 2, Spreadsheet Basics* for instructions on using Excel's **Paste Function** commands).

ANOVA summary table. Figure 11.5 shows the ANOVA summary table for the two-way analysis of variance for independent samples.

- **Source of variation.** The *Total* variation is partitioned to examine the two main effects: the *Sample (Rows)* factor, which is Gender, and the *Columns* factor, which is Expectation. The source of variation labeled *Interaction* refers to the joint effect of the Sample (Row) and Column factor (e.g., the combination of Gender x Expectation). The line labeled *Within* represents the variability that is random or due to sources other than those under investigation in the current study. The *Within* component will provide the denominator for all the *F* ratios generated by the analysis. Notice we have three *F* ratios for any two-factor ANOVA.

- **Interpretation of the *Sample* (Rows) factor.** The observed *F* value for the *Sample* (Rows) factor is found in cell E25 and equals .664. This value is clearly not significant. This observed *F* fails to meet the critical *F* value of 4.35 needed to reject the null hypothesis; its associated *p* value of .425 fails to meet the .05 alpha level. Since this factor represented our gender groups, the analysis is telling us that males ($\underline{M}$ = 19.08) and females ($\underline{M}$ = 19.67) were essentially similar in creativity scores. In other words, there was no main effect for gender.

- **Interpretation of the *Columns* factor.** The observed *F* value for the *Columns* factor is found in cell E26 and equals 29.93. This value is clearly statistically significant. This observed *F* exceeds the critical *F* value of 4.35; its associated *p* value of .0000235 meets the .05 alpha level. (Excel displays very small *p* values in scientific notation, which is the case here. The *p* value for the *Columns* factor is listed as 2.35E-05 in cell F26. E-05 means you must move the decimal place five digits to the left to obtain the real value: *p* = .0000235). To interpret the meaning of this significant *F* ratio, look at the means for each column in Figure 11.4. They tell us that creativity scores were significantly lower when evaluation was expected (*M* = 17.42) than when it was unexpected (*M* = 21.33). In other words, there was a main effect for expectation condition such that expecting an evaluation appears to lower creativity.

Figure 11.5
ANOVA summary table.

	A	B	C	D	E	F	G
23	ANOVA						
24	Source of Variation	SS	df	MS	F	P-value	F crit
25	Sample	2.041666667	1	2.041667	0.663957	0.424764	4.35125
26	Columns	92.04166667	1	92.04167	29.93225	2.35E-05	4.35125
27	Interaction	0.041666667	1	0.041667	0.01355	0.908492	4.35125
28	Within	61.5	20	3.075			
29							
30	Total	155.625	23				

- **Interpretation of the *Interaction*.** The observed *F* value of .014 for the *Interaction* is not statistically significant. There was no difference in how males and females were affected by the two different expectation conditions. That is, both groups reacted similarly and showed less creativity when they were expecting to be evaluated, and more creativity when not expecting an evaluation. *If* the interaction effect had been statistically significant, you would go back to the group means and conduct further analyses to interpret the results.

> **Note of caution:** In interpreting main effects when there are more than two levels or conditions of a factor, you need to use a procedure like the Scheffé test or the Tukey test to determine whether the difference between each mean pair is statistically significant. You need to refer to a statistics textbook for these; Excel does not contain any such statistical techniques. Here, no follow-up procedure was necessary because there were only two levels of each factor: male vs. female for the Sample (Row) factor, and evaluation expected vs. no evaluation expected for the Columns factor.

Step-by-Step Practice Exercise

1. Make up a set of data appropriate for a 2 x 2 factorial ANOVA. You need two levels or conditions for one factor and two levels or conditions for a second factor. The data must come from four separate groups; it cannot involve repeated measurements on the same sample. Use 8 scores in each of the four conditions and label your columns.

2. To the side of your spreadsheet data, type in a brief description of your example and the research hypotheses being tested.

3. Use the **Analysis ToolPak's Anova: Two-Factor With Replication** procedure to perform a two-factor ANOVA for independent samples. Use alpha = .05. Save the output on a new worksheet named *Twofactor*.

4. Beneath the output generated by the procedure, type an interpretation of the results. What did you find out about the relationship between the two independent variables and the dependent variable? For each potential main effect and interaction, include a decision about the null vs. alternative hypothesis, identify the observed *F* value and its associated *p* value, and give the appropriate group means.

5. Save your file using the name *Twofactor*.

12

The Pearson Product-Moment Correlation

The Pearson correlation, the most commonly computed correlation statistic, measures the strength of a relationship between two variables. Correlation is frequently used in the social sciences because the variables in question, such as socioeconomic status or intelligence, cannot be manipulated, but it is also used commonly in laboratory studies where the variables under study *can* be manipulated.

Correlations can be divided into two categories: positive and negative. In a positive correlation, both variables have a tendency to increase together, as in the scatterplot in the left-hand panel of Figure 12.1. This plot shows that deaths among manatees, which are endangered marine mammals, have risen along with the number of boat registrations in Florida. These data were collected over a number of years. In a negative correlation, as one variable increases in magnitude, the other variable decreases in magnitude, as in the scatterplot in the right-hand panel of Figure 12.1. This plot presents hypothetical data that show a negative correlation between per capita fish consumption and death rate from heart disease. Considered country by country, higher fish consumption is associated with fewer heart disease deaths. Notice that for both correlations, the relationships described appear linear. That is, a straight line could be drawn through each point cloud.

Figure 12.1 Examples of positive and negative correlations.

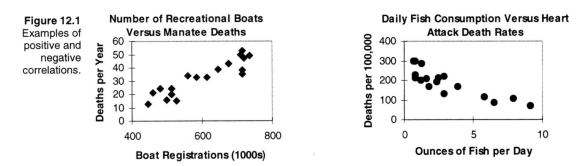

Correlations vary in strength from −1.0 to +1.0. A correlation of -1.0 is perfect, as is a correlation of +1.0. Perfect means that all of the data points fit on a straight line. For example, imagine that a perfect, positive relationship existed between manatee deaths and boat registrations. If it did, all of the points on the graph above would form a straight line ascending from left to right, and the manatee death rate could be predicted exactly from the number of boat registrations. Generally, however, correlations fall somewhere in between the two extremes of −1.0 and +1.0, meaning that the data points are scattered around the line that best describes the relationship.

Excel can perform the work of calculating the Pearson *r* with minimal effort in two different ways. The first way is through the **Paste Function**; the second, through the **Analysis ToolPak**. Excel can also create a scatterplot that will express the data visually.

Obtaining the Pearson *r* with the Paste Function

Excel contains two **Paste Function** commands appropriate for calculating the Pearson correlation: the **CORREL** command and the **PEARSON** command. Both return the same mathematical value; both involve identical steps except for the initial choice of command (**CORREL** or **PEARSON**). We used **PEARSON** here because the command name serves as a reminder of the specific correlation statistic being computed.

Step 1: Enter the Data

Imagine that a psychologist and a sociologist have studied the habits of 20 middle-school children during the summer months. They compiled the average time per day spent watching television, playing video games, or surfing the Internet (video); and the average time per day reading books, in the belief that a tradeoff exists between these two classes of activity.

Enter the data shown in Figure 12.2. Save these data because we will use them again for regression analysis in the next chapter. To save, click on the 💾 icon and fill out the dialog box.

Step 2: Find the Pearson Correlation

- Highlight the cell in which you wish to place the correlation value.
- Open the **Paste Function** menu.
- Choose the **Statistical** category.
- Scroll down the window on the right and select **PEARSON**.
- Enter or highlight the cell range for the data in the **PEARSON** dialog box (shown in Figure 12.3). Enter the cell range for the daily hours of video variable in **Array1**. Do this either by typing in the range or by clicking in the **Array1** box and then highlighting the range with the mouse. Be sure *not* to include the column labels. Click in the **Array2** box and enter the range for daily hours of reading books.
- Click on **OK** and the correlation result will be pasted into the highlighted cell.

Figure 12.2
Data for Pearson correlation exercise.

	A	B
1	Video (hours/day)	Books (hours/day)
2	3.1	2.6
3	4.5	1.6
4	3.5	1.2
5	6.3	0.8
6	3.5	2.1
7	1.4	4.9
8	6.7	1.6
9	0.4	5.1
10	4.3	2.4
11	8.5	0.1
12	5.4	0.6
13	4.4	2.3
14	1.4	2.2
15	7.1	0.6
16	2.2	2
17	6.4	0.2
18	1.9	2.8
19	1.8	3.9
20	9.3	0
21	3.8	3.2

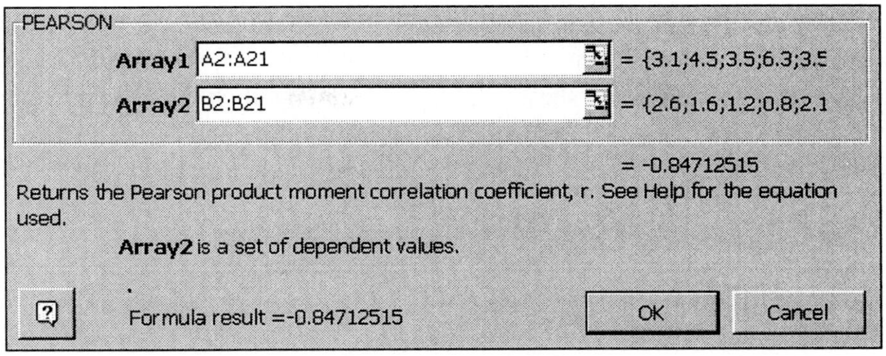

Figure 12.3
Pearson dialog.

PEARSON		
Array1 A2:A21		= {3.1;4.5;3.5;6.3;3.5
Array2 B2:B21		= {2.6;1.6;1.2;0.8;2.1

= -0.84712515

Returns the Pearson product moment correlation coefficient, r. See Help for the equation used.

Array2 is a set of dependent values.

[?]   Formula result = -0.84712515   OK   Cancel

Step 3: Interpret the Results of the Analysis

The value for the Pearson r should be –0.847, provided you entered the data correctly. For this sample, a strong negative relationship exists between time spent watching television or playing video games, and time spent reading books. The observed correlation tells us that there is a tradeoff between these two forms of activity, though it does not tell us how these personal habits developed, nor does it tell us that reading time will automatically increase if parents make new rules that decrease time spent on television or video games. Children may seek out other activities if video time is rationed, but other factors will probably determine whether reading is the alternate activity of choice.

Obtaining the Pearson r with the Analysis ToolPak

Step 1: Enter the Data

The data (see Figure 12.2) are the same as those used for the previous exercise.

Step 2: Choose the Analysis Procedure

- From the **Tools** menu choose **Data Analysis**.
- Scroll down and highlight **Correlation** in the **Data Analysis** dialog box (see Figure 12.4).
- Click on the **OK** button.

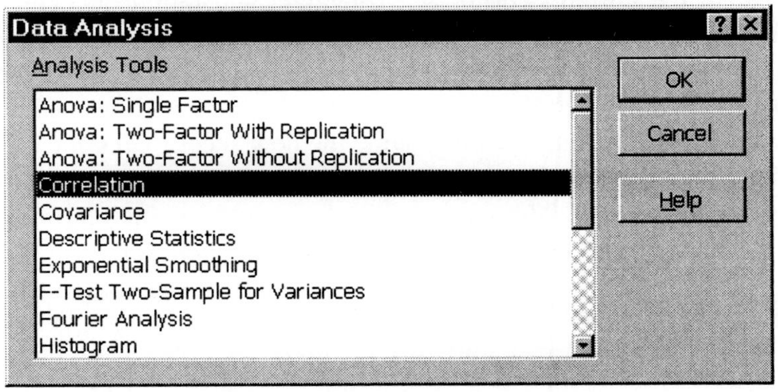

Figure 12.4
Data Analysis
dialog.

Data Analysis	[?][X]
Analysis Tools	OK
Anova: Single Factor	
Anova: Two-Factor With Replication	Cancel
Anova: Two-Factor Without Replication	
Correlation	
Covariance	Help
Descriptive Statistics	
Exponential Smoothing	
F-Test Two-Sample for Variances	
Fourier Analysis	
Histogram	

Step 3: Fill in the Dialog Box

Complete the dialog box shown in Figure 12.5 and click the **OK** button to run the analysis. If you choose to highlight the spreadsheet cells instead of manually typing in the range, Excel adds the dollar signs seen in Figure 12.5.

Figure 12.5
Correlation
dialog box.

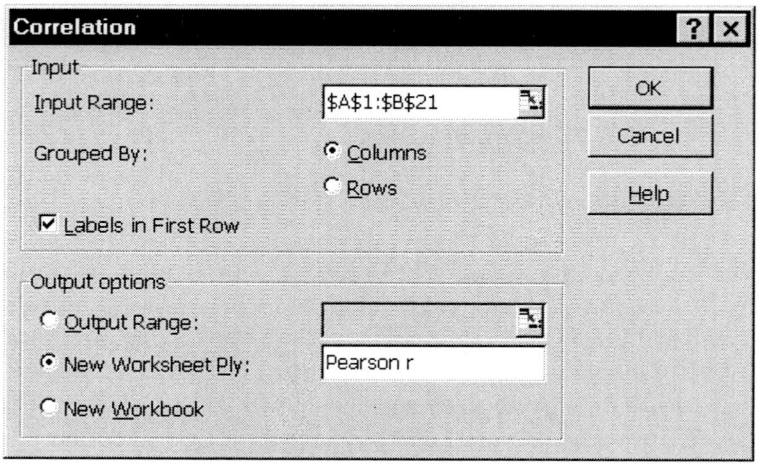

Input Range. Enter the cell locations of all the data, including your variable labels. In this example, the cell range is A1:B21.

Grouped By. Indicate whether the data set for each variable extends down a column or across a row. Data entry in Excel is typically in column format so this is already marked as the default option.

Labels. Be sure to check this box so that your variable labels will be included with the output. Whenever your input range includes the cells containing the names of the variables, you must check the **Labels** box or Excel will give an error message.

Output Options. Excel provides three choices for the output's location:
- **Output Range** places the output on the same spreadsheet page as your original data; you specify the cell location for the upper left corner of the output, e.g. cell D1.
- **New Worksheet Ply** is the default output location. Excel pastes the output into a new worksheet in the current workbook. Your data and output are kept together in the same file. You have the option to name the new worksheet by typing a name into the text box. If you do not name the new sheet, Excel will name it *Sheet 4,* or the next available name in the series (*Sheets 1, 2,* and *3* are created whenever you start a new Excel workbook). For our exercise, name the new sheet *Pearson r.*
- **New Workbook** means Excel pastes the output into a different workbook from the one containing the data. This is probably the least desirable option, as your data and statistical analyses will not be together in the same Excel file.

Tip: When Excel pastes output into a spreadsheet, labels and values in the output may be cut off because the columns are not wide enough. To widen a column, position the mouse pointer over the divider to the right of the column. When the pointer changes to a cross ✚, hold down the primary mouse button and drag the column's edge to the right. Release the mouse button when everything is visible.

Step 4: Interpret the Results of the Analysis

After running the **Correlation** procedure and widening the columns, you should have output that looks like Figure 12.6.

Figure 12.6
Output of the
Correlation
procedure.

	I19	▼	=		Width: 16.67
	A	B	C	┼	D
1		Video (hours/day)	Books (hours/day)		
2	Video (hours/day)	1			
3	Books (hours/day)	-0.84712515	1		

Notice that the **Correlation** procedure has produced three numbers, not just one as the **Paste Function** does. This output is a correlation matrix, in which each variable in the analysis is correlated with every other variable in the analysis. The value $r = -0.847$ is the correlation between video time and reading time. The 1s in the matrix indicate that each variable is perfectly correlated with itself. Producing a matrix for two variables may seem strange, but the technique becomes valuable when you have more than two variables and you want to see all the correlation coefficients simultaneously.

Creating a Scatterplot

A scatterplot is a graph that shows the relationship between pairs of data obtained on two variables (see Figure 12.1). Scatterplots are commonly used to visualize data obtained for a correlation analysis. These graphs aid in determining whether data are linearly related in a positive or negative fashion, or whether data are related in some non-linear fashion. Scatterplots in Excel are usually created through the **Chart Wizard**, although we will explore another way in *Chapter 13, Simple Linear Regression*.

Begin by highlighting the data for inclusion in the scatterplot. Here, the variables are *Video (hours/day)* and *Books (hours/day)* in cells A1:B21 (see Figure 12.2). Remember that a scatterplot shows the relationship between two numerical variables, so you must select only two variables for the chart.

Chart Wizard Step 1: Chart Type

After highlighting your data, activate **Chart Wizard** by clicking the icon ▥ on the **Standard Toolbar** located beneath the menu bar. The **Chart Wizard** displays the first of four dialog boxes. Here you select the type of chart you wish to create (see Figure 12.7).
- Choose **XY (Scatter)** under **Chart type**.
- Use the default scatterplot under **Chart sub-type**.
- Click and hold the **Press and hold to view sample** button to get a chart preview.
- Click on **Next** to bring up Step 2.

Figure 12.7
Chart Wizard
Step 1.

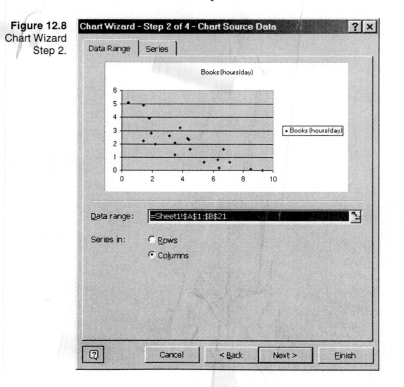

Chart Wizard - Step 1 of 4 - Chart Type

Standard Types | Custom Types

Chart type:
- Column
- Bar
- Line
- Pie
- XY (Scatter)
- Area
- Doughnut
- Radar
- Surface
- Bubble
- Stock
- Cylinder
- Cone

Chart sub-type:

Scatter. Compares pairs of values.

Press and hold to view sample

Cancel   < Back   Next >   Finish

Chart Wizard Step 2: Chart Source Data

When **Step 2 of 4** comes up (Figure 12.8), make sure you have selected the correct data range. If so, click **Next**. If not, refer back to *Chapter 4, Bar and Line Charts,* for further information on this step.

Figure 12.8
Chart Wizard
Step 2.

Chart Wizard - Step 2 of 4 - Chart Source Data

Data Range | Series

Books (hours/day)

• Books (hours/day)

Data range: =Sheet1!$A$1:$B$21

Series in: ○ Rows
● Columns

Cancel   < Back   Next >   Finish

Chart Wizard Step 3: Chart Options

The third step of the **Chart Wizard**, shown in Figure 12.9, presents several tab sheets of options for formatting the chart. Perform the following actions so that the chart will have a polished appearance:

- Replace the default chart title with a more meaningful title. Here, use *Relationship Between Time Spent Watching Video and Time Spent Reading Books.*
- Enter the title for the X-axis: here, *Video (hours/day).*
- Enter the title for the Y-axis: here *Books (hours/day).*
- Choose the **Gridlines** tab. Turn off the gridlines by unchecking **Major gridlines** under **Value (Y) axis.**
- Choose the **Legend** tab. Remove the legend by unchecking **Show legend.**
- Click **Next.**

Figure 12.9
Chart Wizard
Step 3.

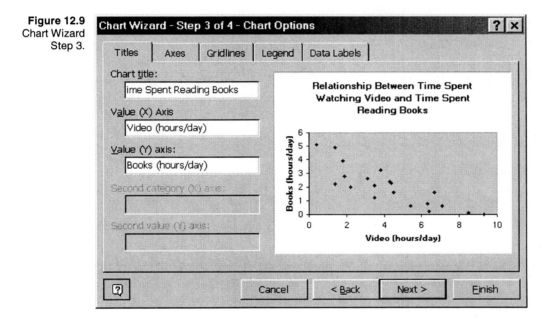

Chart Wizard Step 4: Chart Location

At the final step (Figure 12.10), you choose the destination for the chart. We will save it as a new sheet called *ScatterPlot.*
- Click the **As New Sheet** button.
- Name the new sheet, then click on **Finish.**

Figure 12.10
Chart Wizard Step 4.

Finishing the Scatterplot

Almost any chart element can be customized by double-clicking it, resizing it, moving it, or clicking on it with the secondary mouse button, which will bring up a context menu of formatting choices. At a minimum, you should increase the font size of all text contained in the chart to 14 points so it will appear more suitable for presentation. Refer back to *Chapter 4, Bar and Line Charts,* for instructions on how to change font sizes.

In this chapter, we will introduce one new chart customization method, which is how to change the size and shape of a plotting symbol.

- Double-click on any of the plotting symbols. The **Format Data Series** dialog box should appear, as shown in Figure 12.11.
- Select the **Patterns** tab.
- Under **Marker**, choose a circle in the **Style** dialog box.
- Change the **Foreground** and **Background** to black.
- Change **Size** to 8 pts.
- Click on the **OK** button.

Figure 12.11
Format Data
Series dialog box.

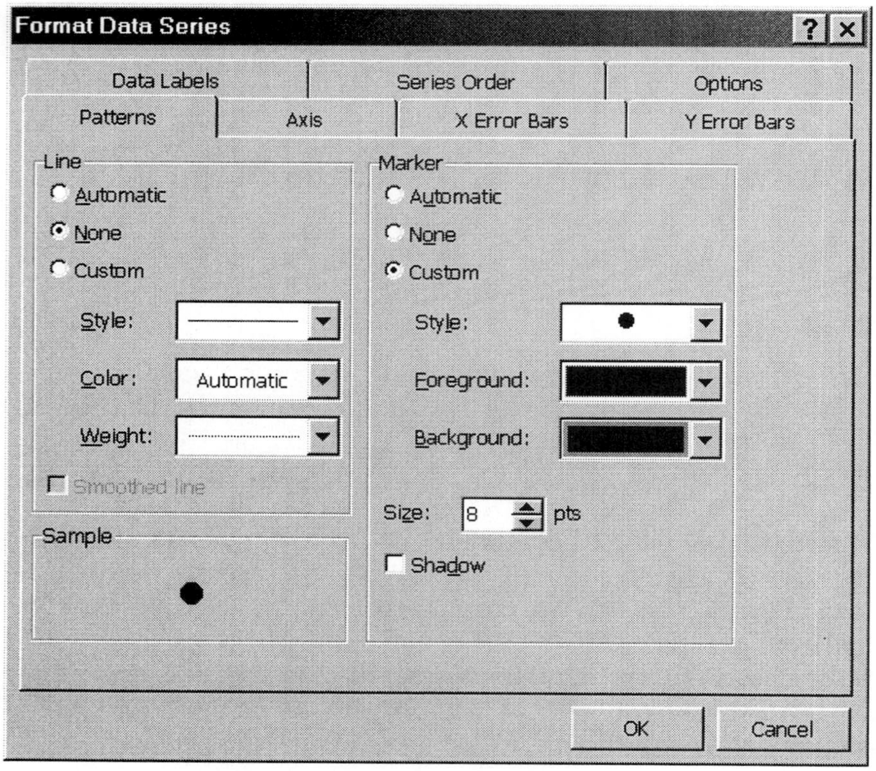

Step-by-Step Practice Exercise

1. Make up pairs of data on two variables that might reasonably be correlated. Use 20 pairs and label each data column.

2. To the side of your spreadsheet data, type in a brief description of your example and the correlation being tested.

3. Use the **Analysis ToolPak Correlation** procedure to find the Pearson correlation between the data, and save this output as a new worksheet named *Pearson*.

4. Beneath the output, write an interpretation of the relationship between the two variables. Is the correlation positive or negative? Is it small, moderate, or large?

5. Return to your original spreadsheet data located in Sheet 1. This time use the **Paste Function** to find the sample mean (**AVERAGE**), sample standard deviation (**STDEV**), and the Pearson correlation (**PEARSON**). Paste the calculated values onto Sheet 1 somewhere near your column of data and label the output.

6. Compare the Pearson correlation answer from Step 3 above with that from Step 5. Did you get the same value? If not, you most likely made a mistake in entering cell ranges for the data. Correct any mistakes before continuing.

7. Create a scatterplot of the data and save it in a new sheet called *Plot*.

8. Save the entire file using the name *Pearson*.

Simple Linear Regression

Regression analysis is intimately related to Pearson correlation, which was described in *Chapter 12*. If two variables are significantly correlated, one can be used to make predictions about the other. One familiar example is the use of SAT scores to predict grade point average in college. The goal of simple linear regression is to find the best-fitting straight line (the regression line) for a set of data made up of X, Y pairs. After the line has been fit, the equation of the line can be used to predict values of Y for given values of X. In other words, for any given SAT score, the regression line would predict a specific grade point average.

Because it is conventional to predict Y from X, X is often called the explanatory variable, or independent variable, and Y is often called the response variable, or dependent variable. Keep in mind, however, that the terms explanatory variable and independent variable are simply convenient labels, and that one cannot establish a causal interpretation based solely upon regression analysis. In fact, in many situations, it makes just as much sense to predict values of X from values of Y.

Figure 13.1
Least squares
solution.

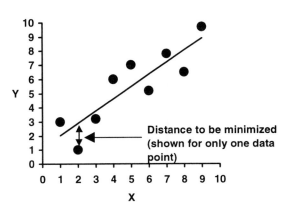

Just as the mean is a measure of central tendency in a single set of scores, the regression line is a measure of central tendency through the data points. To determine the best fitting line, a mathematical procedure is used that determines the distance between the line and each data point along the Y axis (see Figure 13.1). Then the procedure minimizes the total squared distances. Otherwise, as is the case for the mean, the positive deviation scores from the line would cancel out the negative deviation scores. This mathematical procedure is referred to as the least squares solution. The equation of the best-fitting line will have the form of $Y_{predicted} = bX + a$, where b is the slope of the line, and a is the point where the line crosses the Y axis, known as the intercept of the line.

Performing the Regression Analysis

Step 1: Enter the Data

If you saved the data set from *Chapter 12*, load it now by choosing **Open** from the **File** menu, or by clicking on the open 🖝 icon. If not, reenter the data, which is reproduced for you in Figure 13.2. Our regression analysis will give us information about predicting amount of time spent reading books based on knowledge about how much time a person spends using video forms of entertatinment.

Figure 13.2
Data for the regression exercise.

	A	B
1	Video (hours/day)	Books (hours/day)
2	3.1	2.6
3	4.5	1.6
4	3.5	1.2
5	6.3	0.8
6	3.5	2.1
7	1.4	4.9
8	6.7	1.6
9	0.4	5.1
10	4.3	2.4
11	8.5	0.1
12	5.4	0.6
13	4.4	2.3
14	1.4	2.2
15	7.1	0.6
16	2.2	2
17	6.4	0.2
18	1.9	2.8
19	1.8	3.9
20	9.3	0
21	3.8	3.2

Step 2: Choose the Analysis Procedure

- From the **Tools** menu choose **Data Analysis**.
- Scroll down and highlight **Regression** in the **Data Analysis** dialog box (see Figure 13.3).
- Click on the **OK** button.

Figure 13.3
Data Analysis
dialog box.

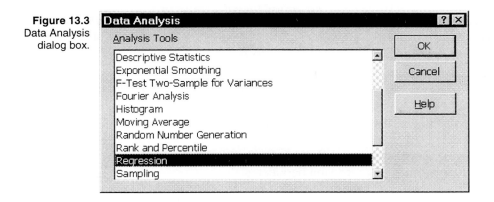

Step 3: Fill in the Dialog Box

Fill in the dialog box shown in Figure 13.4, then click the **OK** button to run the analysis. If you choose to highlight the spreadsheet cells instead of manually typing in the range, Excel adds the dollar signs seen in Figure 13.4.

Figure 13.4
Regression dialog
box.

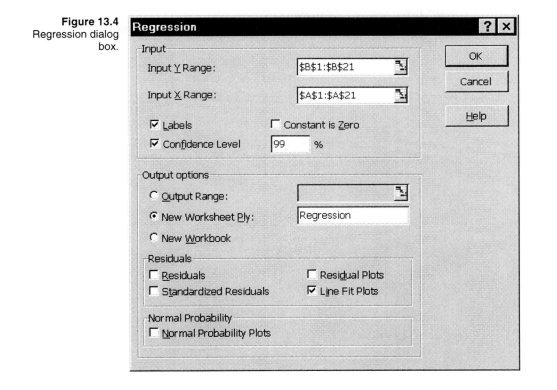

Input Y Range. Enter the cell locations of all the Y data, including the variable label. Remember that Y generally represents the variable that you wish to *predict to*, often called the dependent variable. In this example, the Y data are in the *Books (hours/day)* column (B1:B21).

Input X Range. Enter the cell locations of all the X data, including the variable label. Remember that the X variable generally represents the variable that you wish to *predict from*, often called the independent variable. In this example, the X data are in the *Video (hours/day)* column (A1:A21).

Labels. Be sure to check this box so that your variable labels will be included with the output. Whenever your input range includes cells containing the names of the variables, you must check the **Labels** box or Excel will give an error message.

Confidence Level. Excel's behavior is unusual here; it automatically calculates two redundant 95% confidence intervals for each regression parameter, even if this box is not checked. For one of the two confidence intervals to be something other than 95%, check this box and enter a different confidence level. For this exercise, we will specify a 99% confidence level. Therefore, we will obtain both a 95% confidence interval and a 99% confidence interval for each regression parameter.

Output Options. Excel provides three choices for the output's location:
- **Output Range** places the output on the same spreadsheet page as your original data; you specify the cell location for the upper left corner of the output, e.g. cell D1.
- **New Worksheet Ply** is the default output location. Excel pastes the output into a new worksheet in the current workbook. Your data and output are kept together in the same file. You have the option to name the new worksheet by typing a name into the text box. If you do not name the new sheet, Excel will name it *Sheet 4,* or the next available name in the series (*Sheets 1, 2* and *3* are created whenever you start a new Excel workbook). For our exercise, name the new sheet *Regression.*
- **New Workbook** means Excel pastes the output into a different workbook from the one containing the data. This is probably the least desirable option, as your data and statistical analyses will not be together in the same Excel file.

> **Tip:** When Excel pastes output into a spreadsheet, labels and values in the output may be cut off because the columns are not wide enough. You may need to widen the columns. Position the mouse pointer over the divider to the right of the column to be widened. When the pointer changes to a cross ✛, hold down the primary mouse button and drag the column's edge to the right. Release the mouse button when everything is visible.

Residuals. The term residuals refers to the deviation scores of each predicted Y from each observed Y. The output from the regression analysis will provide a table of residual scores regardless of whether you mark the **Residuals** checkbox. **Standardized Residuals** provides the normalized residuals (the residuals converted to z-scores). **Residual Plots** plots the unstandardized residuals against the X data. **Line Fit Plots** draws a scatterplot of the data, including the best fitting line. Check only **Line Fit Plots** for our exercise.

Normal Probability. Checking this box will provide a normal probability plot of the data. We will not use this option in our example.

Step 4: Interpret the Results of the Analysis

After completing Step 3 and widening the columns, you should have output that looks like Figure 13.5. (Use the zoom control 75% ▾, on the **Formatting ToolBar** to see all the data at once, or scroll using the arrow tabs.) The output is grouped into five different categories: *Regression Statistics, ANOVA, Parameter Estimates, Residuals,* and *Line fit Plot.* You will need to resize the *Line Fit Plot* so it is easier to read. In the next section, we will examine each category in detail.

Figure 13.5
Output of the
regression
procedure.

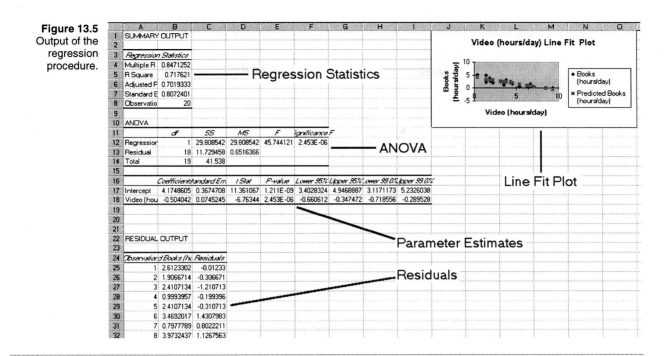

Detailed Examination of the Regression Output

Regression Statistics

Figure 13.6
Detail of the
regression
statistics.

Regression Statistics	
Multiple R	0.847125
R Square	0.717621
Adjusted R Square	0.701933
Standard Error	0.80724
Observations	20

The regression statistics produced by Excel are shown in Figure 13.6:

- **Multiple R** ($r = 0.85$, rounded) is equivalent to the absolute value of the Pearson correlation observed between book time and video time. Since this value will always be positive, despite the fact that we have a negative correlation in our example, you must remember to provide the sign when reporting the Pearson r value. From Excel's total regression output, there are two ways to determine the actual direction of the correlation: (1) Examine the line fit plot to see whether the scatterplot shows a positive or negative correlation; (2) examine the parameter estimates to find the value of the slope, b. A positive slope means a positive correlation; a negative slope means a negative correlation.

- **R Square** (0.72, rounded) is the same as the product r^2, which provides an estimate of the proportion of variance in time spent on reading that is explained by variation in time spent on video (or vice versa). Put another way, **R Square** reflects the amount of variance X and Y have in common.

- **Adjusted R Square** is used in multiple regression analyses; we will ignore this value as our focus is simple linear regression.

- **Standard Error** (.807) is the standard error of estimate, which is a measure of the typical, or average, deviation of individual observations (X, Y pairs) from the regression line.

- **Observations.** Examine this value to ensure that all of the data have been analyzed. In our example, we had 20 pairs of observations.

ANOVA

Figure 13.7
Detail of the
ANOVA output.

ANOVA

	df	SS	MS	F	Significance F
Regression	1	29.80854	29.80854	45.74412	2.45257E-06
Residual	18	11.72946	0.651637		
Total	19	41.538			

Figure 13.7 shows the analysis of variance (ANOVA) summary table:
- **SS Regression** (29.809, rounded) is the sum of squares (SS) based on the correlation between X and Y (video time and book time).
- **SS Residual** (11.73, rounded) is the sum of squares due to random variation (i.e., due to sources other than the correlation between X and Y). SS residual is equal to the sum of the squared deviations of the actual scores on Y from their corresponding predicted scores on Y (which come from the regression line).
- **SS Total** (41.54, rounded) is the total sum of squares found by adding SS Regression and SS Residual. Notice that the SS Regression divided by the SS Total is equal to r^2.
- **F ratio** (45.74, rounded) is obtained by dividing MS_{reg} by MS_{res}. The statistical significance of the F ratio in Figure 13.7 is displayed in scientific notation, so you have to mentally convert the displayed value to .00000245, or reformat the cell to display eight or more decimal places. Since the obtained probability is much less than alpha = .05, we will conclude that the regression of book time on video time is significantly different than zero, meaning that the relationship observed between book time and video time is probably not due to chance.

Parameter Estimates

Figure 13.8
Detail of the
parameter
estimates.

	Coefficients	Standard Error	t Stat	P-value	Lower 95%	Upper 95%	Lower 99.0%	Upper 99.0%
Intercept	4.1748605	0.367470814	11.36107	1.21E-09	3.402832412	4.946889	3.11711727	5.23260382
Video (hours/day)	-0.504042	0.074524507	-6.76344	2.45E-06	-0.660612336	-0.347472	-0.7185565	-0.2895276

- **Slope and Y-intercept coefficients.** Figure 13.8 shows the Excel output related to estimating the slope and Y-intercept of the regression line. The coefficients for our regression equation, $Y_{predicted} = bX + a$, are Y-intercept (a) = 4.175 (rounded), and slope (b) = -.504 (rounded). This means the specific regression equation for our data is: $Y_{predicted} = -5.04X + 4.175$.
- **Standard error of the coefficients.** The slope and the Y-intercept are both estimators of their corresponding population parameters. Hence, each has an associated standard error. Do not confuse these standard errors with the standard error of estimate, which is an index of error in predicting scores on Y. The standard error of the intercept (s_a) is .3675 and the standard error of the slope (s_b) is .0745.
- **t Stat.** The t statistic associated with the regression coefficients is a test of whether each coefficient differs significantly from zero. The degrees of freedom for each test are $n - 2$. For our example, the Y-intercept differs significantly from zero, $t(18) = 11.36$, $p < .00000000121$, as does the slope, $t(18) = -6.76$, $p = .00000245$.
- **Confidence intervals.** These are calculated based on the t distribution with $n - 2$ degrees of freedom. With 95% confidence, the parameter for the Y-intercept lies within

the range 3.403 to 4.947, and the parameter for the slope lies within the range -.661 to -.347. As with the *t* test, one may also conclude from these intervals that the estimated population parameters do not include zero, with 95% confidence. A similar interpretation applies to the 99% confidence intervals.

Residuals

The residual output shown in Figure 13.9 consists of three columns. The first column, labeled *Observation*, indicates to which data point (X, Y pair) the row refers. *Predicted Books* contains the predicted value of Y for each observed X, found by using our regression equation, $Y_{predicted} = -5.04X + 4.175$. The third column, *Residuals*, contains the deviation of each predicted Y from each observed Y. For example, for observation 1, the observed Y was 2.6, but the predicted Y was 2.612, which means the prediction was slightly in error.

Figure 13.9
Detail of the residual output.

RESIDUAL OUTPUT

Observation	Predicted Books (hours/day)	Residuals
1	2.612330232	-0.012330232
2	1.906671383	-0.306671383
3	2.410713418	-1.210713418
4	0.999395719	-0.199395719
5	2.410713418	-0.310713418
6	3.469201693	1.430798307
7	0.797778905	0.802221095
8	3.973243728	1.126756272
9	2.00747979	0.39252021
10	-0.109496759	0.209496759
11	1.453033551	-0.853033551
12	1.957075586	0.342924414
13	3.469201693	-1.269201693
14	0.596162091	0.003837909
15	3.065968064	-1.065968064
16	0.948991515	-0.748991515
17	3.217180675	-0.417180675
18	3.267584878	0.632415122
19	-0.512730387	0.512730387
20	2.259500808	0.940499192

Line Fit Plot

The line fit plot shows the predicted value of Y for each value of X. Unless you have resized your line fit plot to look like Figure 13.10, it will be compressed and difficult to read. To resize:
- Click on the plot with the primary mouse button; eight square *handles* appear around the plot area.
- Place the mouse pointer over one of the handles so that the pointer changes to a resizing arrow (↕, or ↘).
- Hold the primary mouse button down and drag to the desired size. (Selecting one of the corner handles will allow you to resize both the vertical and horizontal axes simultaneously).

Figure 13.10
Line fit plot after resizing.

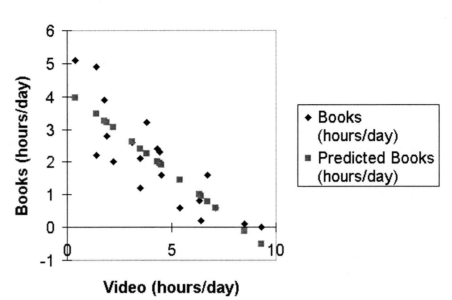

Customizing the Line Fit Plot

Adjust the Line Style

Traditionally, the best fitting line is shown as a solid line through the point cloud in the scatterplot. To achieve this:

- Click on one of the data points on the line. Square handles should appear on the entire data series.
- Double-click on the same data point to bring up the **Format Data Series** dialog box, shown in Figure 13.11.
- For **Marker**, select **None**.
- For **Line**, select **Custom**, a color of your choice, and check **Smoothed line**.
- Click the **OK** button.

Figure 13.11
Format Data Series dialog box.

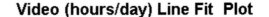

Adjust the Scale

The Y-axis should start at zero rather than minus one.

- Double-click on the Y-axis to bring up the **Format Axis** dialog box (Figure 13.12).
- Select the **Scale** tab.
- Change the **Minimum** value to 0.
- Click the **OK** button.

Change the Title

The default graph title is not very informative.

- Click on the title with the primary mouse button. Eight square handles will appear.
- Click once on one of the words in the title by using the primary mouse button.
- Edit the title when a vertical, blinking edit cursor appears. Here, use *Relationship Between Time Spent Watching Video and Time Spent Reading Books*.
- Click the **OK** button

Figure 13.12
Format Axis dialog box.

Format Axis ? X

| Patterns | Scale | Font | Number | Alignment |

Value (Y) axis scale

Auto

☐ Mi<u>n</u>imum: 0

☑ Ma<u>x</u>imum: 6

☑ Ma<u>j</u>or unit: 1

☑ M<u>i</u>nor unit: 0.2

☑ Value (X) axis

  <u>C</u>rosses at: 0

☐ <u>L</u>ogarithmic scale

☐ Values in <u>r</u>everse order

☐ Value (X) axis crosses at <u>m</u>aximum value

[OK] [Cancel]

Change the Plot Background

Change the background of the plot area from gray to white so that it will reproduce better on black and white printers.

- Double-click in the gray chart area. The **Format Plot Area** dialog box appears.
- Either select **None** under **Area**, or click on white as the area fill color.
- Click the **OK** button.

Final Touches

You can perform many more customizations by double-clicking any chart element, including labels, axes, lines, and symbols, to bring up a dialog box. After you are finished customizing, you should have a chart that looks something like the one in Figure 13.13.

Figure 13.13
Line fit plot after
customization.

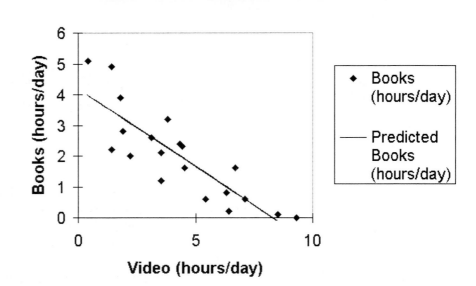

Figure 13.13
Line fit plot after customization.

Step-by-Step Practice Exercise

1. Make up pairs of data on two variables that might be positively correlated. Use 20 pairs and label each data column.

2. To the side of your spreadsheet data, type in a brief description of your example and the regression being performed.

3. Use the **Analysis ToolPak Regression** procedure to perform the regression analysis. Be sure to click the **Line Fit Plots** option. Direct the output to a new worksheet named *Regression*.

4. Write a brief description of what the output means somewhere in the visible portion of the sheet named *Regression*.

5. Customize the line fit plot so that the output looks more acceptable. At the very least, resize the plot and make the best-fitting line a solid line rather than a series of dots.

6. Save the entire file using the name *Regression*.

Exchanging Files Between Excel, SPSS, and Other Applications

Excel itself is not a full-fledged statistical application, nor was it designed to be. More advanced users may need to conduct analyses that go beyond Excel's basic capacities. Therefore, it is advantageous to know how files created in Excel can be imported into and exported from widely used statistical programs like SPSS (Statistical Package for the Social Sciences). Because data entry is simpler in Excel, some users prefer to create files in Excel and later import them into a statistical package for analysis. Other users may have files originally created in SPSS or another application that they wish to use in Excel.

In order to accommodate all these users and applications, we have divided this appendix into two sections. The first describes how to open files in another program when they have been saved in Excel's native file format (*.xls). Because of Excel's popularity, many current applications (e.g., SPSS, SYSTAT, MINITAB, Lotus, Quattro Pro) include the capacity to read Excel files directly. Still, not all existing applications include this feature. Therefore, the second section describes how to exchange files between Excel and other applications using a generic file format (*.txt or *.dat) that is based on an encoding scheme called ASCII (American Standard Code for Information Interchange). These files, often called text files, can be read by any statistical, spreadsheet, or database application. In both sections we illustrate the file exchange process between Excel and SPSS, which is one of the most commonly used statistical packages. Knowledgeable readers who wish to exchange files between Excel and an application other than SPSS should be able to generalize from the instructions provided here.

Because this book is essentially a guide to doing statistics with Excel, it is not our purpose to instruct users in SPSS. References to the specifics of data analysis in SPSS are kept to a minimum, but we assume the reader has some familiarity with statistical applications like SPSS. The reader should note that SPSS 8.0 for Windows 95 was used for all screen shots and instructions, though our experience is that the file exchange process is similar in SPSS 6.0 for Windows.

WORKING WITH NATIVE EXCEL FILES

Importing Native Excel Files from Excel into SPSS

As with most software, there are multiple ways to carry out a desired task. The easiest way to read a native Excel file in SPSS is to save it as an Excel 4.0 file, as described in the steps that follow. Although SPSS can read native Excel file types newer than version 4.0, doing so involves a complex process using a **File** menu feature in SPSS called **Database Capture**.

Step 1: Enter the Data in an Excel Spreadsheet

For our example, let us suppose that a sociologist has survey data on a large sample, including demographic information on gender, race, age, and years of formal education. Enter the small portion of data shown in Figure A.1 as you normally would in Excel, with each variable in its own column.

Tips:
- Unlike Excel, SPSS restricts variable names to 8 characters. If you use column headings longer than 8 characters, the names will be truncated when you import the file into SPSS.
- We chose to enter gender and race as text (string) variables. We could just as easily have entered them as numeric variables, with 1 as a numeric code for the category *male* and 2 as a numeric code for the category *female.*

Figure A.1
Survey data.

	A	B	C	D
1	Gender	Race	Age	Educate
2	female	white	62	12
3	male	white	31	20
4	female	white	35	20
5	female	white	27	19
6	female	black	25	12
7	male	other	59	11
8	male	black	46	10
9	female	other	55	16
10	female	black	57	11
11	female	white	64	14
12	male	black	72	9
13	female	white	67	12
14	male	white	33	15
15	male	other	22	14

Step 2: Save the File as an Excel 4.0 Worksheet

- Click on Excel's **File** menu.
- Choose **Save As.**
- Fill in the **Save As** dialog box (see Figure A.2). Choose a location to store the file (**Save in**) and type a **File name**. For our example, type in the filename *demograph spss.*
- Click on the arrow in the **Save as type** box.
- Scroll down the file types to select **Microsoft Excel 4.0 Worksheet**.
- Click the **Save** button.
- Ignore the warning that appears telling you that the selected file type does not support workbooks containing multiple sheets (see Figure A.3). This warning appears even if you *do not* have multiple sheets in your data file.

- Click **OK** and the save operation will be complete.

Tip: If you have a very large Excel file with data in more than 256 columns, you will need to save the file as text (tab-delimited) to import it into SPSS. See the section titled *Working with ASCII Text Files* later in this appendix.

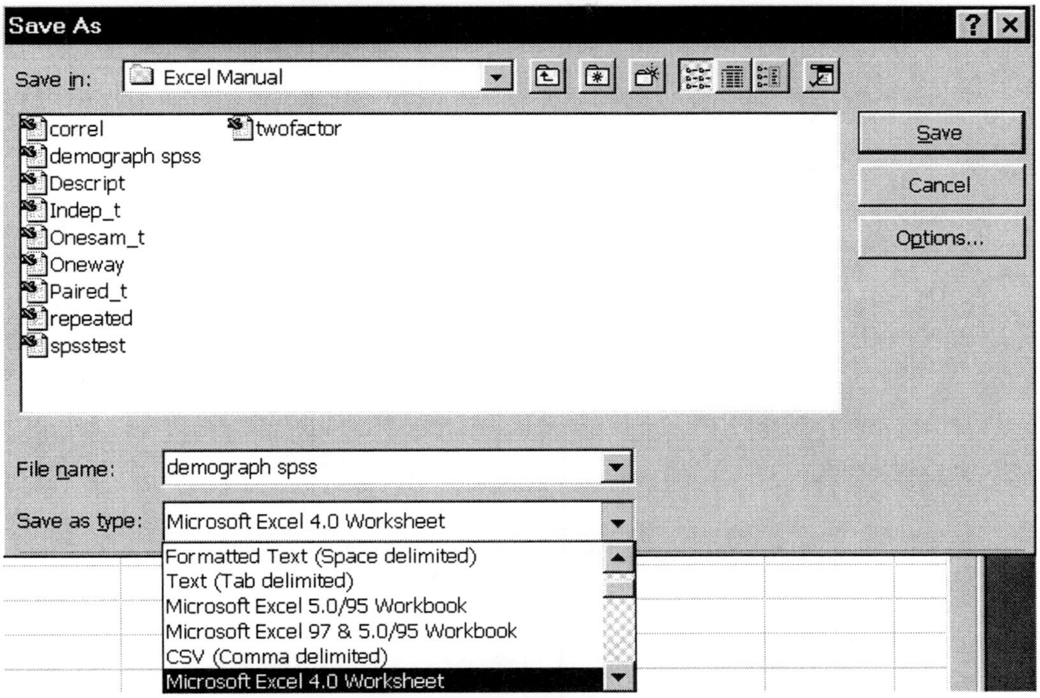

Figure A.2
Save As dialog box.

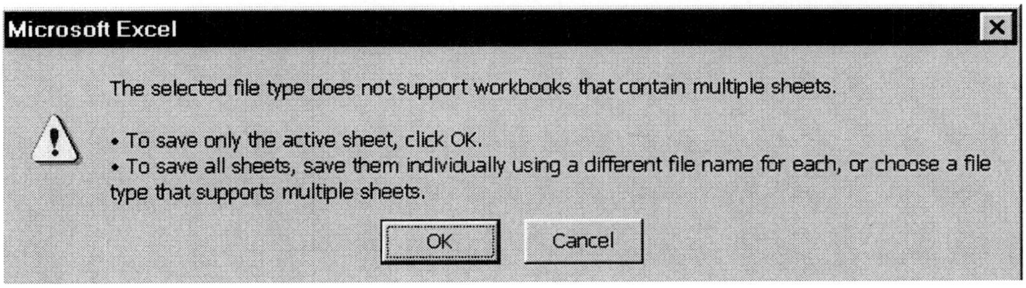

Figure A.3
This Excel warning can be ignored.

Step 3: Open the Excel 4.0 File in SPSS

- Start your SPSS application (version 8.0 for Windows 95 is shown in Figure A.4).
- Click on the SPSS **File** menu.
- Choose **Open**.
- When the **Open File** dialog box shown in Figure A.5 appears, click on the arrow in the **Look in** box. Navigate to where your data file is stored.
- Click on the arrow in the **Files of type** box.
- Scroll down the list and highlight the file type, **Excel (*.xls)**. A list of all Excel files stored in the location will appear in the window (see Figure A.5). Do not be fooled into thinking you can easily open any native Excel file! If you attempt to open an Excel file other than one saved as version 4.0 (or an earlier version), SPSS will display a message that you must save the file as Excel 4.0.

- Select the file *demograph SPSS*, which we saved in Excel 4.0 format during Step 2.
- Click on the **Open** button.

Figure A.4
SPSS 8.0 for
Windows with File
menu dropped
down.

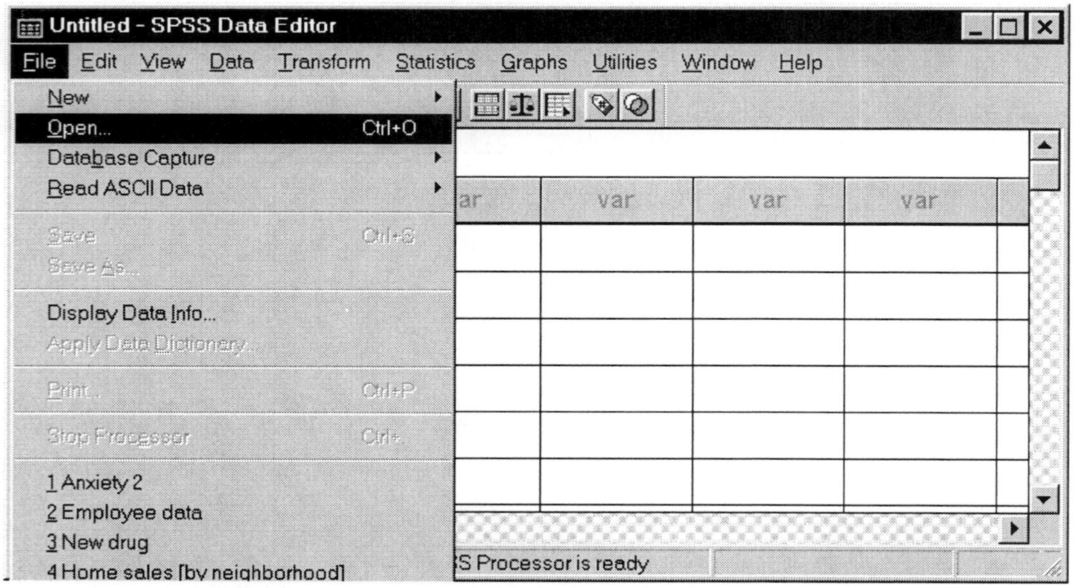

Figure A.5
Open File dialog
box showing list
of Excel files.

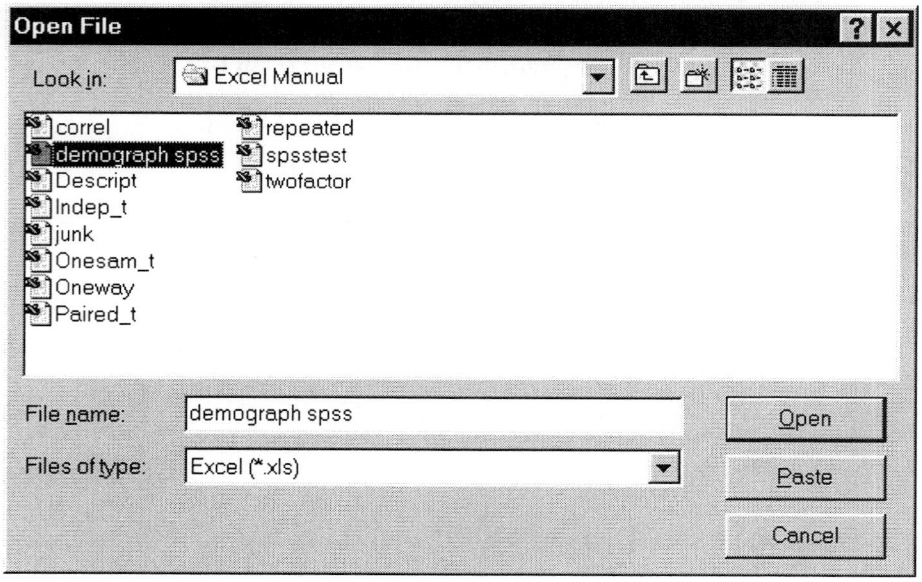

- When SPSS displays a dialog box of **Opening File Options** (see Figure A.6), put a check in the box labeled **Read variable names**. This insures that SPSS will import the original column headings from the Excel file.
- Enter the **Range** of cells where the data and headings are located in the Excel spreadsheet. Be careful here. A common mistake is to enter the incorrect cell range. Our demographic data file spans the cell range A1:D15. You can enter a wider range than necessary (e.g., A1:D20), but if you completely forget to enter a cell range, you will receive an error message and SPSS will be unable to import the file.
- Click on the **OK** button.

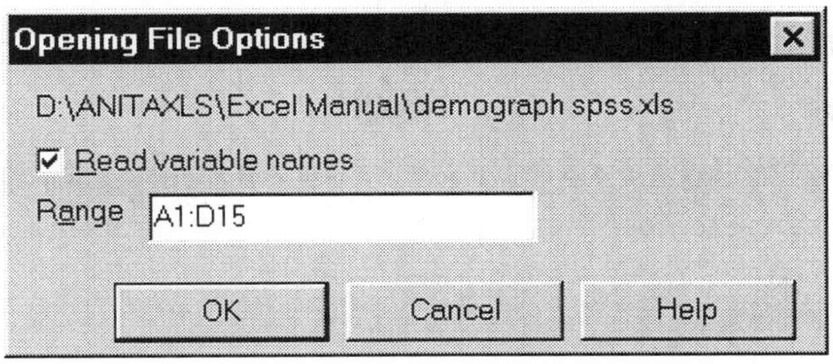

Figure A.6
Opening File
Options dialog
box.

Immediately after completing these actions, SPSS opens the file in its **Data Editor** (see Figure A.7) and simultaneously generates an output file (see Figure A.8). The output file shows the variable names, types, and number of cases read, such as that created for our demographic data. You may examine the output file to insure the data were correctly imported, but there is no need to save it, so simply close this file.

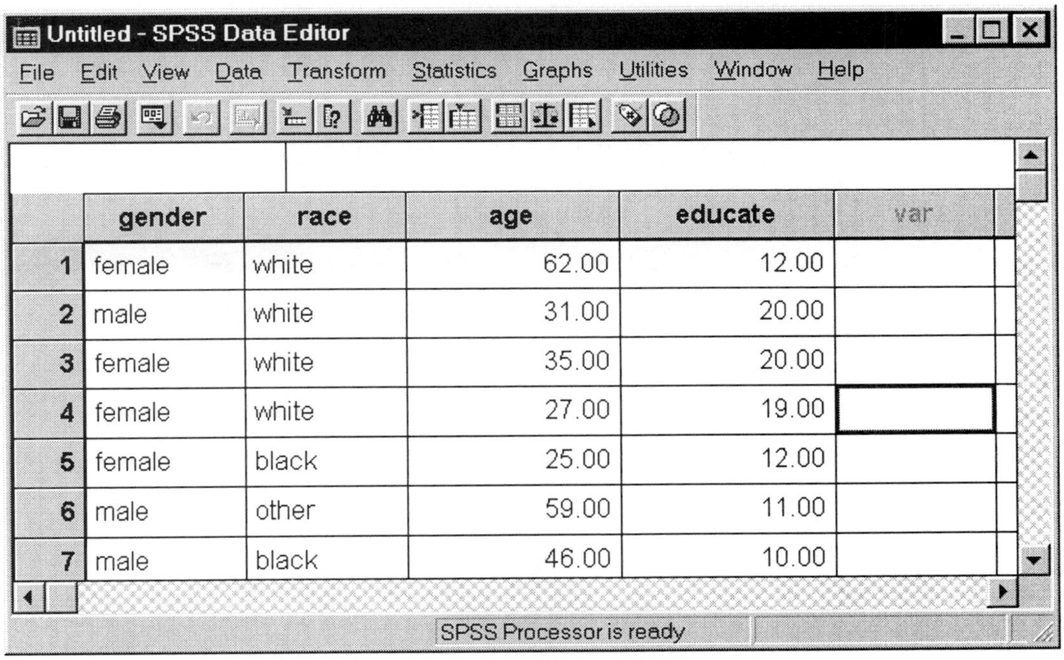

Figure A.7
SPSS 8.0 Data
Editor.

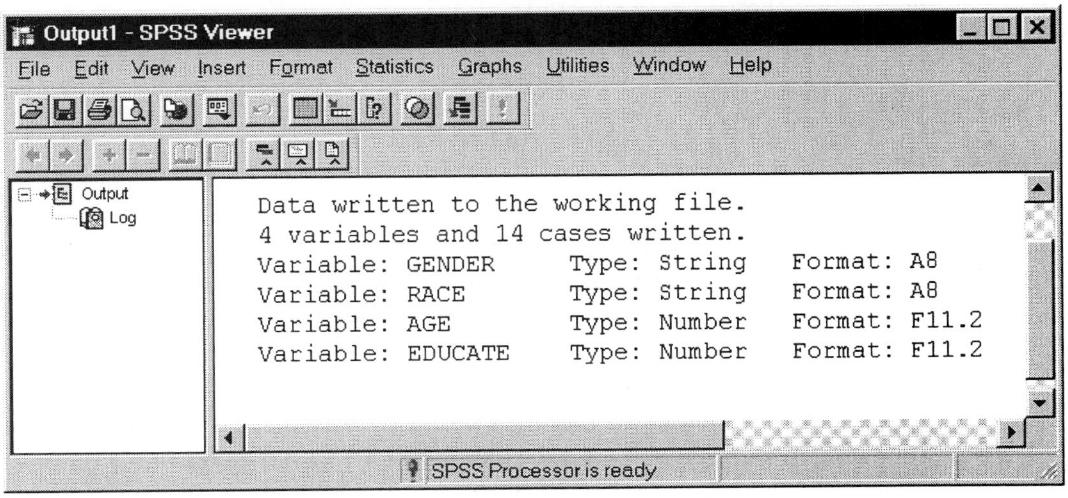

Figure A.8
Output file
summary
information.

Exporting Native Excel Files from SPSS for Use in Excel

SPSS can save files in native Excel format (*.xls), which is useful when you have files originally created in SPSS that you wish to use in Excel. The process is similar to the one just described for converting Excel files to version 4.0 format for use in SPSS.

Step 1: Enter the Data in SPSS

Assume we have data from a personnel office about a person's gender, salary, and address.

- Start SPSS.
- Enter the data shown in Figure A.9 into the SPSS **Data Editor**. For this exercise, we assume you already know how to use the **Data menu** and can define variables in SPSS.

Figure A.9
Data in the SPSS
Data Editor.

	gender	salary	address	var
1	m	77000.00	111 Wall St	
2	f	54000.00	222 Madison Ave	
3	f	33000.00	333 Overseas Highway	
4	m	39000.00	444 JFK Boulevard	
5	m	24000.00	555 Lover's Lane	
6	f	41000.00	666 Devil's Way	
7	f	38000.00	777 Las Vegas Strip	
8	m	49000.00	888 Fairway Drive	

Step 2: Save the SPSS Data in Native Excel Format

- Click on the SPSS **File** menu.
- Select **Save As**.
- Fill in the **Save Data As** dialog box that appears (see Figure A.10). Choose a location to store the file (**Save in**) and type a **File name.** Here, we used the filename *salary*.
- Click on the arrow in the **Save as type** box.
- Scroll down the file types and select **Excel (*.xls)**. Notice that beneath the **Save as type** selection area there is a check box labeled **Write variable names to spreadsheet**. If this box is checked, the SPSS variable names will appear as column headings in the Excel spreadsheet. SPSS should automatically have this option checked, but if for some reason it is not, make sure you click in the box to turn this feature on.

- Click the **Save** button to finish the operation.

After saving the file, SPSS will generate an output file describing the conversion process that has just occurred. You may examine the output file to insure the data were read correctly, but there is no need to save it, so simply close the file.

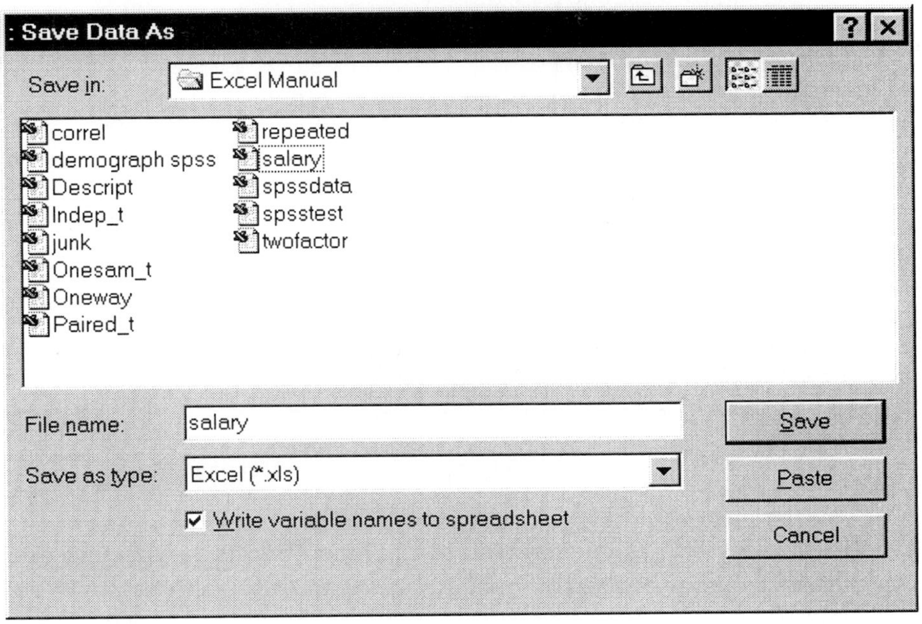

Figure A.10
Save Data As
dialog box.

Step 3: Open the *.xls File in Excel

- Start Excel.
- Click on Excel's **File** menu and choose **Open**.
- Fill in the **Open File** dialog box (refer back to Figure A.5). Use the **Look In** arrow to navigate to the location where you stored the file. Select the appropriate filename, which in this case is *salary*.
- Click **OK**; the contents of the original SPSS file will appear in Excel, as shown in Figure A.11.

Tip: You may need to widen a column to see all the data. For instance, in opening the *salary* file in Excel, pound signs were displayed instead of salary figures, as shown below.

	A	B	C
1	GENDER	SALARY	ADDRESS
2	m	######	111 Wall St
3	f	######	222 Madison Ave

The correct salary data appear as soon as you widen the salary column, as shown in Figure A.11.

Figure A.11
The salary data
loaded into Excel.

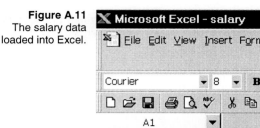

	A	B	C	
1	GENDER	SALARY	ADDRESS	
2	m	77000.00	111 Wall St	
3	f	54000.00	222 Madison Ave	
4	f	33000.00	333 Overseas Highway	
5	m	39000.00	444 JFK Boulevard	
6	m	24000.00	555 Lover's Lane	
7	f	41000.00	666 Devil's Way	
8	f	38000.00	777 Las Vegas Strip	
9	m	49000.00	888 Fairway Drive	

WORKING WITH ASCII TEXT FILES

The process of reading and writing ASCII text files is very similar to the process just described for exchanging files that are in native Excel format. Therefore, we will at times refer back to the previous section and its figures. Excel can work with three types of text files: tab-delimited, space-delimited, and comma-delimited. These file types differ in terms of whether the file is encoded with tabs, commas, or spaces separating the row and column data values. SPSS reads and saves tab-delimited files, so we will use this option for our examples.

Importing Text (Tab-delimited) Files from Excel into SPSS

Step 1: Enter the Data in an Excel Spreadsheet

- Enter the data shown back in Figure A.1 as you normally would, or if you saved *demograph spss* from our previous exercise, open this file in Excel.
- See Step 1 in the previous section for tips on the length of variable names in Excel versus SPSS.

Step 2: Save the File as Text (Tab-delimited)

- Click on Excel's **File** menu.
- Choose **Save As.**
- Fill in the **Save As** dialog box (refer back to Figure A.2). Choose a location to store the file (**Save in**) and type a **File name.** For our example, type in the filename *demographics.*
- Click on the arrow in the **Save as type** box.
- Scroll down the file types and select **Text (tab-delimited).**
- Click the **Save** button.

- Ignore the warning that appears telling you that the selected file type does not support workbooks containing multiple sheets (refer back to Figure A.3). This warning appears even if you *do not* have multiple sheets in your data file.
- Click **OK** and the save operation will be complete.

Step 3: Open the Text (Tab-delimited) File in SPSS

- Start your SPSS application.
- Click on the SPSS **File** menu (refer back to Figure A.4). Note that the SPSS **File** menu has a choice called **Read ASCII Data**. This is a cumbersome import method that you don't need to use if your files are in tab-delimited format.
- Choose to **Open** a file.
- When the **Open File** dialog box appears (refer back to Figure A.5), click on the arrow in the **Look in** box. Navigate to where your data file is stored.
- Click on the arrow in the **Files of type** box.
- Scroll down the list and highlight the file type: **tab-delimited (*.dat, *.txt)**. A list of all ASCII data and text files stored in the location will appear in the window.
- Select the file *demographics*, which we saved in tab-delimited format during Step 2.
- Click on the **Open** button.
- When SPSS displays a dialog box of **Opening File Options** (see Figure A.12), put a check in the box labeled **Read variable names**. This insures that SPSS will import the original column headings from the file you created in Excel. Notice that the **Range** box is grayed out. Unlike files in *.xls format, no cell range needs to be entered with tab-delimited files.
- Click on the **OK** button.

Figure A.12
Opening File Options dialog box.

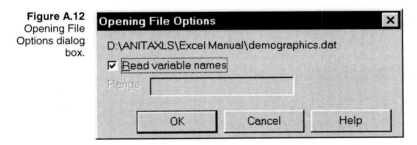

After opening the file, SPSS will generate an output file (shown in Figure A.8) describing the conversion process that has just occurred. You may examine the output file to insure the data were read correctly, but there is no need to save it, so simply close the file.

Exporting Tab-delimited Files from SPSS for Use in Excel

Step 1: Enter the Data in SPSS

- Start SPSS.
- Enter the data shown in Figure A.9 into the SPSS **Data Editor,** or if you saved *salary* from a prior example, open this Excel file in SPSS. For this exercise, we assume you already know how to use the **Data menu** and can define variables in SPSS.

Step 2: Save the SPSS Data in Tab-delimited Format

- Click on the SPSS **File** menu.
- Select **Save As**.
- Fill in the **Save Data As** dialog box shown in Figure A.13. Choose a location to store the file (**Save in**) and type a **File name.** Here, we used the filename *salary*.
- Click on the arrow in the **Save as type** box.
- Scroll down the file types and select **Tab-delimited (*.dat)**. Notice that beneath the **Save as type** selection area there is a check box labeled **Write variable names to spreadsheet**. If this box is checked, the SPSS variable names will appear as column headings in the Excel spreadsheet. SPSS should automatically have this option checked, but if for some reason it is not, make sure you click in the box to turn this feature on.
- Click the **Save** button to finish the operation.

Figure A.13
Save Data As
dialog box.

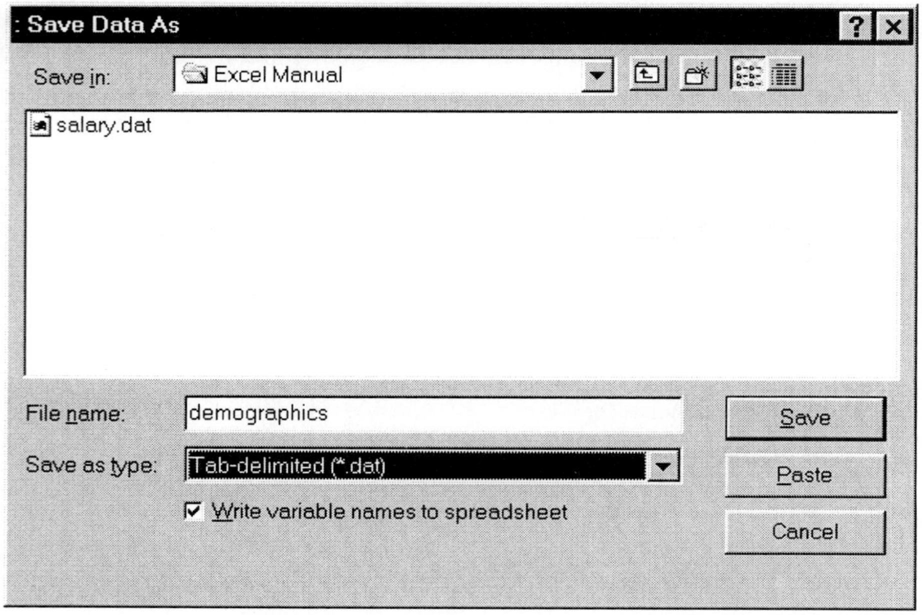

Step 3: Open the Tab-delimited File in Excel

- Start Excel.
- Click on Excel's **File** menu and choose **Open**.
- Fill in the **Open File** dialog box shown in Figure A.14. Use the **Look In** arrow to navigate to the location where you stored the file.
- Click on the arrow in the **Files of type** box.
- Scroll down the list and highlight the file type: **All files**. A list of *all* files stored in the location will appear in the window. You can recognize tab-delimited files created and saved in SPSS because they have a *.dat extension.

Tip: Do not choose **Text Files** from Excel's **Open File** dialog box (see Figure A.14), even though this may seem logical. This choice will not display or open SPSS tab-delimited files.

- Select the file *salary.dat*, which we saved in tab-delimited format during Step 2.
- Click on the **Open** button.
- A three-step **Text Import Wizard** is initiated. Click on **Next** to accept the wizard's suggestions for Steps 1 and 2, then click on **Finish** at Step 3. Your tab-delimited file will be imported into Excel flawlessly. Column width should not even need to be adjusted; identifying column width is done by the **Text Import Wizard**.

Figure A.14
Open dialog box with Files of type list dropped down.

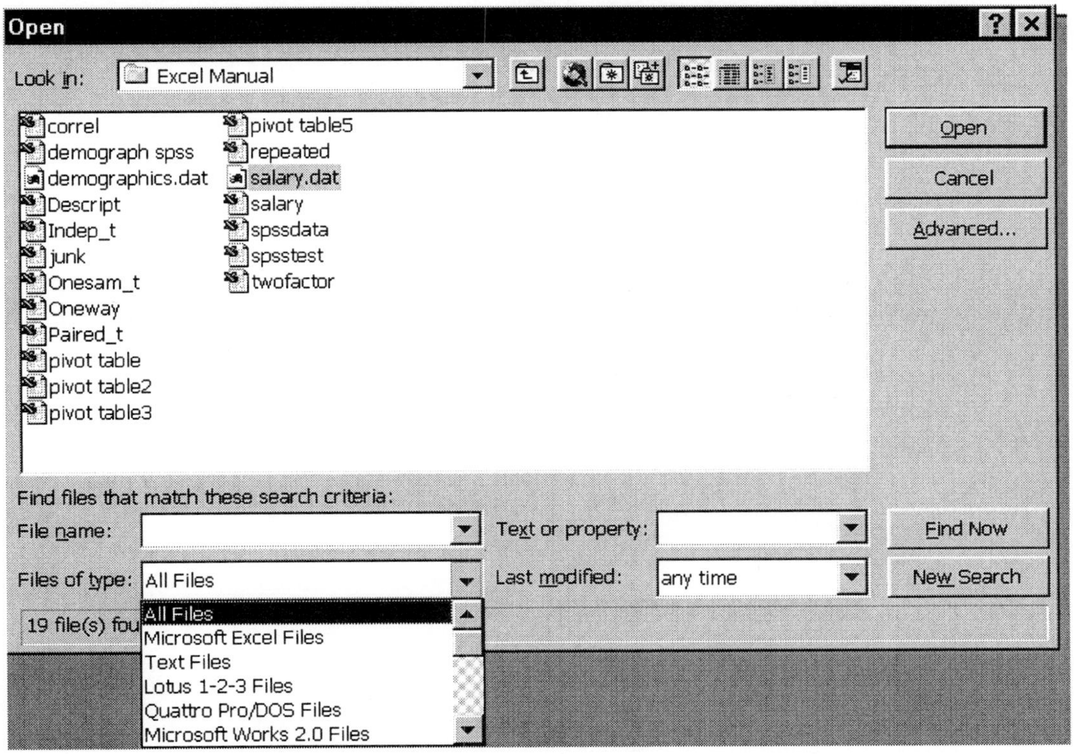

Step-by-Step Practice Exercise

1. To import a native Excel file into SPSS, first open a new Excel spreadsheet. In Columns A and B enter variable labels and 5 data cases. Still within Excel, save the file in Excel 4.0 format using the name *xls4data*.

2. Start your SPSS program and open the *xls4data* file. Close the output file generated by SPSS.

3. To export a native Excel file from SPSS, first start your SPSS application and create an SPSS data file. Include at least two variables of five cases each.

4. Still within SPSS, save the data as an Excel file type using the name *spssxls*. Close the output file generated by SPSS.

5. Start Excel and open the file *spssxls*. If necessary, adjust column widths to see all data.

Note: If you prefer to work with tab-delimited files, perform steps 1-5 but save the file you create in tab-delimited format using the name *spssdata*.

B

Glossary

This glossary is meant to serve as a quick reference for many Excel, Windows, and computer terms used in this book; it does not contain definitions of statistical terms and concepts.

Analysis ToolPak. Excel contains a special set of built-in procedures for data analysis. The ToolPak must be custom-installed for it to appear as an option under the **Tools** menu. See *Chapter 1* for installation instructions.

ASCII. American Standard Code for Information Interchange; a computer coding scheme where alphanumeric and other characters are assigned a standard integer code between 0 and 255.

Chart Wizard. This Excel feature provides a step-by-step series of dialog boxes to walk the user through the creation of numerous types of graphs and charts. Its icon is located on the **Standard Toolbar** (see Figure B.1).

Context menu. When an item is highlighted and you click on the secondary mouse button, a pop-up menu appears with specific options available for manipulating the selection. In other words, the menu is tailored to the highlighted item.

Extension. These are the three characters following the period in a file name. They identify the file type and the original (native) application that created the file. For example, Excel files are saved as .xls, text files as .txt, and SPSS tab-delimited data files use .dat.

Formula Bar. This area, located above the column headers in an Excel spreadsheet (see Figure B.1), shows you the complete formula or contents of a highlighted cell. For example, cell A8 may display the value 12, while the formula bar shows **=SUM(A2:A6)**, indicating that the contents of cells A2 to A6 were added to obtain the value for cell A8.

Function Wizard. In versions of Excel earlier than Excel 97, this was the name of the **Paste Function** command (see definition). The icon f_* and location on the **Standard Toolbar** (see Figure B.1) remain the same across versions.

Native file. A file encoded in a format original to the application that created it.

Output. The results (tables, graphs, and calculations) generated by an analytic procedure.

Paste Function. This Excel command, with its icon f_* located on the **Standard Toolbar** (see Figure B.1), calls up an extensive menu of common mathematical, statistical, and engineering calculations. The dialog box helps the user perform the calculation and paste the answer into the spreadsheet, but is not set up like a "wizard" that methodically walks the user through steps.

Primary mouse button. For most individuals, this is the left mouse button. For left-handers who have reversed buttons for the sake of comfort, this is the right mouse button.

Secondary mouse button. For most individuals, this is the right mouse button. For left-handers who have reversed buttons for the sake of comfort, this is the left mouse button.

Standard Toolbar. This is a row of icons used to perform typical operations such as opening, saving, and printing files; it is located below Excel's main **Menu Bar** (see Figure B.1). The standard toolbar icons will be present unless a user has customized toolbars and intentionally turned this option off.

Tab or **Tab Sheet.** Like a large notebook or binder, Excel and Windows both use dividers or tabs to separate pages. Excel worksheet tabs, for example, are shown in Figure B.1.

Tab-delimited file. This is a specific type of text or ASCII file that both Excel and SPSS can read and write. Tabs are used as separators (delimiters) between row and column data. This generic file type facilitates file exchange between Excel, SPSS, and other applications.

Text file. Any file saved in a format that contains only plain text. Most text files contain the 256 ASCII (American Standard Code for Information Interchange) character set. A text file can be understood by any spreadsheet, statistical, or database software, which facilitates file exchange between Excel and other applications.

Workbook. In current versions of Excel, each new file created is a workbook, which is an electronic equivalent of a notebook. Like a notebook, a workbook can contain many different individual sheets: sheets with data, charts, or reports.

Worksheet. This is a subset of a workbook file and generally refers to the actual spreadsheet work area of rows and columns. In Excel 4.0 and earlier, each file could contain only a single worksheet. Figure B.1 shows a blank worksheet.

Figure B.1
Components of Excel.

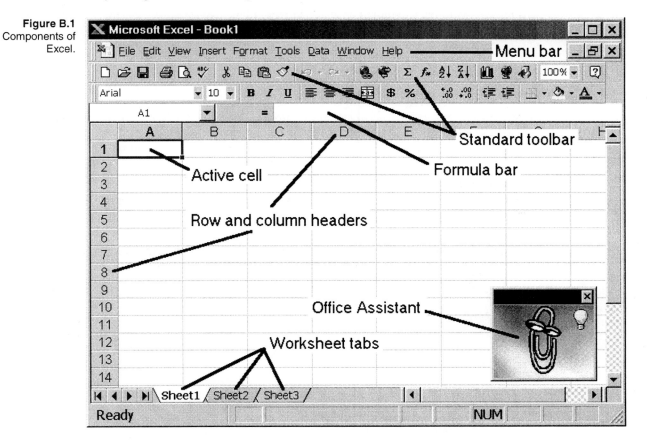

Index